How to Communicate With Your Daughter

The 6 Fundamental Steps in Re-discovering How to Talk to Your Daughter

Carole E Brown

© **Copyright 2022 - All rights reserved.**

The content contained within this book may not be reproduced, duplicated or transmitted without direct written permission from the author or the publisher.

Under no circumstances will any blame or legal responsibility be held against the publisher, or author, for any damages, reparation, or monetary loss due to the information contained within this book, either directly or indirectly.

Legal Notice:

This book is copyright protected. It is only for personal use. You cannot amend, distribute, sell, use, quote or paraphrase any part, or the content within this book, without the consent of the author or publisher.

Disclaimer Notice:

Please note the information contained within this document is for educational and entertainment purposes only. All effort has been executed to present accurate, up to date, reliable, complete information. No warranties of any kind are declared or implied. Readers acknowledge that the author is not engaged in the rendering of legal, financial, medical or professional advice. The content within this book has been derived from various sources. Please consult a licensed professional before attempting any techniques outlined in this book.

By reading this document, the reader agrees that under no circumstances is the author responsible for any losses, direct or indirect, that are incurred as a result of the use of the information contained within this document, including, but not limited to, errors, omissions, or inaccuracies.

Table of Contents

Introduction 5
Step 1: What You're Experiencing 12
    A Mother's Perspective 12
    Things Before and Now 16
    Motherly Instinct 21
    Modeling Respect 27
    In Summary 30
    Application Workbook 1 31
Step 2: Understanding Your Daughter 33
    Through her Eyes 34
    Adolescence 37
    Brain Development 41
    Emotions and Mental Health 44
    Her Priorities 48
    In Summary 51
    Application Workbook 2 52
Step 3: Her Circle of Influence 54
    Her Circle 55
    Patterns and Routines 60
    Expressing Oneself 63
    Bad Influences and Bullying 66
    Attraction and Finding Love 71
    In Summary 74
    Application Workbook 3 75
Step 4: Key Issues Today 76
    Being Perfect 77
    Lack of Motivation 80

Dangers of Helicopter Parenting 84
Self-Esteem, Anxiety, and Depression 85
Mood Disorders 88
Substance Abuse 92
In Summary 94
Application Workbook 4 95

Step 5: Connection 97
What is Connection? 98
Time 102
Going on Dates 106
Understanding their Interests 109
Managing Conflict 112
In Summary.. 116
Application Workbook 5 117

Step 6: Working Together 118
Power of Listening Effectively 119
Judge Less 122
More Supporters, Not Dictators 125
Boundaries VS Free Reign 127
Teach Life Skills 130
Unconditional Love 134
In Summary.. 137

Conclusion 139
References: 143

Introduction

If there is one lesson that I have learned from my 25 years as a relationship coach, it's this: learning to communicate with a teenager daughter is more an art. It's a science.

Over the last quarter-decade, I have encountered the same problem again and again. Mothers have come to me, desperate for answers on how their precious baby girl seemed to transform overnight, turning from their best friend into what feels like an enemy. They describe their problems, their conflicts, and how their worst fights seem to spring from the most mundane moments.

Almost always, these tearful conversations go the same way.

Picture this: A girl—thirteen years old, dressed in her favorite oversized sweater and converses—comes home from school. Her mother is waiting in the living room, still in the process of unwinding from her own hectic workday. The mother gives a greeting, and the daughter nods on her way to the kitchen.

The daughter drops her bag on the floor as she starts digging through the cabinet for her usual snack. Her mother comes in behind her.

"How was your day?"

"Fine."

The mother waits for more details, but they don't come. She decides to risk prodding the beast by asking again.

"Anything interesting happen?"

"No."

The girl's mother is just getting ready to ask another question—maybe about her daughter's friends or a class she has been having difficulty with—when she notices the footprints leading across the white linoleum to where her daughter now stands. She moves to get a broom, then stumbles over the backpack her daughter left lying in the middle of the floor.

Suppressing a curse, the mother says, "How many times have I asked you not to throw your stuff in the middle of the walkway?"

The daughter rolls her eyes and says, "I'll get it in a minute."

"No, you'll get it now. Any clean up that mud you tracked in while you're at it."

"Okay, Carol," the girl says, knowing how her mother hates being called by first name, "Can't I at least eat first?"

Carol rubs her temples, already preparing for the headache that is sure to come. After a long day, she is exhausted, irritable, and not in the mood to relive yet another tense battle they've had a thousand times before. It was such a long day. When her boss had been particularly hard on her after a minor mistake, her nosy coworkers had been all too happy to see it unfold. The car has been making that strange noise again, and she is worried that she might have an expensive bill the next time she takes it in to the shop. She is physically and mentally exhaustion, and after a long afternoon on her feet, she would kill to just sit down and order pizza.

That's not in the cards tonight, though. Sarah has soccer tomorrow, which means they'll be ordering from a drive-through then. The idea of eating unhealthy slop two days in a row makes her feel like she's failing at her job as "mom." She feels like that a lot lately. Between work, the messy house, and the constant pressure of maintaining the perfect "mother" image, she feels as if she's being pulled in one hundred directions at once. She cannot remember the last time that she had a moment to herself; Of course, unless you counted the few nights a week she stayed up well beyond her usual bedtime, just grateful to have a moment alone.

As the mother goes to the refrigerator for a diet Pepsi, she reminds herself: this will all be worth it.

She thinks back to when Sarah was just a girl, all excitement and blonde curls and pigtails. In those days, they were absolute partners in crime, the best friends imaginable. Whenever Carol went to work, she spent all day looking forward to the moment she pulled up at Sarah's elementary school to see her running up the sidewalk. Sarah would fling open the car door and jump in place, already mid-sentence as she described every single thing she had seen, done, or tasted throughout the day.

In those days, even "temper tantrums" were manageable, easily solved with a hug, a few words, and maybe a treat. When Sarah got in trouble back then, she actually *apologized* after. Whenever Carol heard the other moms on the playground complaining about their whiny daughters, she'd had to hide a smile of superiority. She felt invincible; she felt like "supermom."

Now, she takes a long sip of water and holds in the sigh she doesn't want her daughter to see. *It's going to be fine*, she tells herself. *You can do this. You can hold it in. You're doing this for Sarah.*

Carol looks back at Sarah just in time to see those big brown eyes roll towards the back of her head one more time. She has to physically bite her tongue as she holds onto the last remaining shreds of her patience.

Just then, the dog comes barreling into the room, his normally white fur stained brown. The mother can feel her blood pressure rising with every breathe.

"Did you leave the front door open again?"

The fight that ensures is par for the course. Carol tells her daughter she doesn't know how she could be so careless. Sarah screams back that it was just an accident, that they happen all the time. Carol tells her that this is the problem, that they happen all the time.

Which quickly turns into a conversation about how it's not Sarah's fault that she can't be as perfect as her older sister. Carol doubles down, saying that she never had this problem with Fiona, that Fiona always emptied the dishwasher the minute she got home.

Sarah calls Fiona the "golden child."

Carol tells Sarah to calm down.

Sarah calls her mom a cruel name.

Carol screams at her to go to her room.

Sarah slams the door behind her so hard that the pictures shake on the walls.

Carol fixes the dinner she had planned, but no one enjoys it. Just like the day before, they eat their meals in complete silence, each afraid to speak to the other for fear of what might be said next.

If their situation feels familiar, don't worry; you're not alone. All too easily, mothers and daughters experience communication breakdowns exactly like this, leading to fractioned, tense relationships they never thought they would have to endure. They may find themselves feeling as if they are enemies more often than family, as if every interaction is a mine field. On the worst days, they may worry that they are doomed to repeat this same pattern again and again until finally, one of them leaves the house.

Luckily, this is far from the case.

The goal of this guide is simple: to help ease tension within mother-daughter relationship and solve the most common issues that lead to this manner of problems. In this book, you will learn how to better understand and interact with one another. With the help of some easy guides, exercises, and activities, you'll have no issue coming to learn from one another's perspectives and repair the tension that may seem unending throughout your home.

In the coming chapters, you'll learn:

- How to be less judgmental of your daughter's decisions and choices
- How to balance both boundaries and freedom
- How to support her in solving her own problems
- How to better focus on listening to her instead of speaking at her
- How to release control when you worry about her decisions
- How to identify problems areas on communication
- How to come to maintain patience in the face of defiance
- How to support your daughter in becoming the best version of herself
- How to defuse conflicts and feel closer to each other

At this point, you may be wondering: are Carol and Sarah real people?

In a way, yes.

Carol and Sarah are the culmination of every mother and daughter I have successfully coached from heartbreak into happiness. Through their experiences, I hope to help others skip past the pain and start the valuable work of repairing what, for many, is the most important relationship in their lives.

Are any two relationships the same? Absolutely not. Do all mothers and daughters carry the same issues? No way! But with love, care, and the proper steps, there is no hurt or resentment that is beyond fixing.

Step 1: What You're Experiencing

Let's face it: sometimes, teenagers can be real jerks.

Seemingly powered by hormones and emotion, they rage through our homes in a constant state of annoyance, ready to roll their eyes at any given moment. As the mother of a teen or tween daughter, you've likely become all too accustomed to feeling as if you are talking to a wall. You may often feel overwhelmed, or as if you are doing an awful job in the most important role that you've ever had. Like Carol, you may feel like every interaction is building towards a losing battle.

In your darkest moments, you may worry that your own daughter is on her way to hating you.

The purpose of this chapter is to shine a light on the psychology behind the emotions you are experiencing, as well as to show how you are not alone. Within these pages, we will explore the history behind motherly intuition and the science behind parenting. Though there is no "one sized fit all" solution to most parenting problems, we will explore strategies that can easily become a part of your normal routine, nurturing a way into a healthy, respectful relationship with your daughter.

A Mother's Perspective

Let's return to Carol and Sarah once more.

After their largest, most recent fight, Carol did her best to hide all that she is feeling; it wouldn't do anyone any good. She went through the motions of washing up after dinner, started a load of laundry, and settled down on the couch beside her husband, Tom. If he noticed the tension in the household since he got home, he hadn't said anything. He may have learned from experience not to bring it up. The idea made Carol even sadder. After only a few minutes of watching television, Carol couldn't focus any longer. She stood up, squeezed Tom's hand for good luck, and walked to Sarah's room.

Sarah lay flopped stomach-first onto her bed, headphones in her ear. Though she seemed to be scrolling through her phone, her eyes were unfocused. They were also a little puffy as if she had just finished crying. When Carol opened the door, Sarah looked up with a glare and rolls over.

"Can we talk?" Carol asked.

After a moment's hesitation, Sarah adjusted on the bed to face her mother. She slowly pulled one earbud out of her ear. Carol took that as a sign of victory.

"Are you okay, bug?"

Sarah shrugged, staring down angrily at the carpet. Carol waited for an answer that didn't come.

Carol continued, "Do you think you'd want to go out for a bit? Maybe go get ice cream? I think Marble Slab Creamery might be open until nine."

A few years ago, these words would have been enough to send Sarah jumping in place for excitement. In her current mood, she just shrugged.

"I'm not in the mood," she said.

"What's wrong? Is it school?"

Sarah glared back at her mother, and Carol had to bite her tongue to stop the remark on the edge of her lips.

"Why does it always have to be something? Why can't I just not be in the mood?" Sarah spat. Before Carol could tell her to stop with the "back talk," Sarah turned her back to her mother and plugged the headphone back into her ear. When Carol turned to leave, the last thing she heard is Sarah asking her to shut the door on the way out.
Carol fought a childish urge to slam it.

As she walked back down the hall, a strange mix of anger and sadness brewed in her heart, she glanced at the framed picture of Sarah on the wall. In this picture, Sarah is still just a child, maybe four or five years old. Her hair is pulled back in a ribbon on the top of her head, but Carol can see that it's in the process of falling. Sarah is gripping the side of the swing set in both hands, grinning up at the photographer with a look of unbridled joy in her eyes.

Carol remembered the very minute she took that photo.

It was a Saturday in the middle of summer. Carol had just gone back to work after taking a break when Sarah was born, and the transition had been jarring. After being accustomed to spending every waking minute with Sarah, every minute they had together felt precious. Glad for a sunny day, Carol had taken Sarah to the playground five miles from their house for an early afternoon filled with sunshine and laughter.

From the way Sarah had acted on that day, you might have thought that she had never been let out of the house before.

Every kid she ran into was her best friend. Every dog was the "most beautiful thing" she'd ever seen, and she wasn't shy about telling the owners. Every piece of playground equipment was the most fun, most amazing thing she had ever touched. By the time Carol was ready to take Sarah home, the girl was covered in sand and could not keep the smile from her face for a single minute.

On her way off the playground, Sarah let go of her mother's hand for just a moment. She wrapped her tiny palms around the leg of the swing set—how could such tiny hands even exist?—and used her body weight to spin herself around and around. As if her body could no longer contain the joy she felt, she burst into a song about how this was the best day ever.

Carol picked up her camera just in time to capture the moment.

Less than a decade later, Carol looked at that precious little girl and wondered what happened. She felt as if her heart would never stop aching as she stared at that photo, at that sweet little girl she worried may be gone forever.

Things Before and Now

One of the most overwhelming parts of parenting a teenager is the memory of how much easier things used to feel.

If you're like most mothers, you found the problems in your relationship with your daughter did not start until right before she hit puberty. Until she was in upper elementary school, your daughter likely may have seemed willing to do whatever it took to earn your praise, love and affection. She may have turned to you for everything in life, looking at you as if you were her greatest hero and truest idol. When that little girl gazed up at you, you might have actually felt it might be true.

There is a very good reason for this: as a child, she was physically, mentally, and chemically very different than the person she is today.

As an example, let's turn back to Carol and Sarah.

When Sarah was in infancy, she was totally dependent on her mother. Matters of genetics aside, every part of her seemed completely fresh and ready to mold. Whenever Carol looked at her, she saw more than just a culmination of all her and her husband's love. She saw a beautiful, fragile creature dependent on her for everything. As Carol stared into those large, trusting eyes, she found it difficult to pull her eyes away, and her mind flooded with an urgency to protect this delicate little person, no matter the cost.

What Carol was feeling is a sensation known as synchronization, a sensation when two things or people operate at the same rate.

According to research published in the Proceedings of the National Academy of Sciences, whenever an adult maintains eye contact with an infant, a type of special bond is formed. The longer they stare, the more the neural pathways of these two people are likely to connect, leading to advanced levels of nonverbal communication (Leong).

That feeling you may have gotten that you and your baby daughter shared a connection that went below skin level? It's true!

Through this mental synchronization, babies can more safely, and quickly navigate their way through the world. When Carol stared into baby Sarah's eyes, she was actively shaping the way she communicated with the world around her. When she sang that nursery rhyme, she was increasing the chances that Sarah would be able to happily relate to others.

Fast forward a few years, and Sarah became a toddler. As she ventured through the world, growing bolder with every day, she began developing her unique personality. For the first time, she began to feel a sense of self and started pushing her boundaries. Carol dealt with growing pains, including tantrums, bursts of energy, mood swings, and attitude.

However, though Sarah was just starting to learn who she was as a person, she still depended on her mother for everything. Even during the long days, Carol found a sense of security in that idea. Though her baby girl was growing, she still had that childish yearning to please. She still turned to her mother at the end of the day and begged for another hug, another bedtime story. When toddler Sarah began to find her words, she used them to tell Carol she loved her.
Parenting at this phase was exhausting but rewarding. When she disciplined her daughter, she did so with the knowledge that she was doing so to keep her safe.

Skip ahead a few more years, and Sarah entered preschool. These were the fun years. At this point, Sarah was starting to grow in independence, but she had yet to pull away. Still a baby in many ways, Sarah turned to Carol for everything.

Now, however, she did so with a sense of awareness, actively asking her mother about the world. Carol's days became filled with questions: "why is the sky blue?" "why is Daddy so much taller than you?" "where do bubbles go?" Though these endless questions often leave Carol feeling overwhelmed, she answers as honestly as she can.

Around ages four and five, children reach the peak levels of curiosity, asking an average of seventy-three questions per day (Independent Digital News and Media). The reason for this is vitally important. As they are striving for independence, their minds are hungry for knowledge, eagerly searching for signs of how the world around them operates. Once again, everything about their psychology points them toward their parents, the people they are most likely to view as the keeper of answers.

Up until this point in Sarah's life, she had been completely dependent on Carol for all the information she receives. All that began to change when she reached elementary school. At this point, Sarah began forming other vital relationships in school, and suddenly her view of the world didn't seem as clear. She came home with strange ideas, leaving Carol scrambling to find where they came from. Instinctively, Carol wanted to trap her daughter in a bubble and protect her from the world, but she knew that couldn't be the answer. Instead, she let her go forth, and all the while, she prayed that nothing would pull her too far away.

By the time puberty hit, all these conflicting ideas about the world reached their peak. Combined with a hurricane of hormones, it should come as no surprise when Sarah begins withdrawing.

Though teenagers are still children in many ways, their psychology works in a far different way. By the time they reach twelve or thirteen years of age, their minds are battling against a thousand different influences as they begin to experiment with what roles they want to take in the world.

In other words, the differences between rearing a child and raising a teen are innumerable. Even the most experienced parents often feel as if they are starting from scratch and parenting a new person altogether.

As a mother, you come blessed with the benefit of time. A separate party to the massive growth that is happening in your daughter's life, you may feel as if she somehow flew through these stages in the blink of an eye. The thought of losing the child you fell in love with may even induce feelings of sadness or grief.

If so, let those emotions come; there is nothing wrong with them whatsoever.

Just as your daughter's race to adolescence is a completely natural part of life, so are the complicated feelings you may have around it. On days when you find yourself missing the innocent girl your daughter used to be, take a moment to remind yourself that all the hardships your daughter is enduring right now are just a step on her journey to becoming who she is meant to be.

Motherly Instinct

Intuition is truly remarkable.

For most people, intuition is an inherent part of who they are. That funny tickle in their gut helps guide them through life, warning them of possible dangers and helping them gauge whether or not the people they meet can be trusted. A vital part of survival, this intuition—also known as "instinct" or "gut feeling"—has helped humanity throughout history, guiding us on our journey through life.

As a mother, your own instinct is likely even more highly tuned than the average person's. Motherly instinct is not just a mommy-blog catchphrase; it's a very real part of human history!

Because infants and children are so highly dependent on their mothers for survival, we as mothers developed an innate sense of what is happening around us. Just as every species on Earth learned skills to help them survive, mothers became highly attuned to the signs of danger that might exist all around us. As a result, our brains began working on overdrive, always paying attention to the tiny details in the background that might signal what is to come next.

This high level of "attention to detail" plays out in ways we might never expect.

Do you ever find yourself unconsciously pushing back a cup that you expect to fall off the edge of the table? Or thinking to yourself, "I think my kid is having a bad day," just for them to walk through the door crying seconds later? Even on your most distracted days, do you somehow know exactly where your daughter left her lost soccer bag in the corner of the laundry room?

This is not a coincidence. It's your inherent motherly instinct in action.

At times, your highly attuned motherly instinct might leave you feeling slightly magical. You may feel gifted as if you are somehow able to see into the future. In a way, you can!

However, this gift does come with a catch: if not nurtured and fully understood, this "gift" can twist into something that often feels like more of a curse, leaving you feeling anxious, stressed, and perpetually overwhelmed.

This issue comes in two parts: putting your senses into overdrive and absorbing your daughter's emotions.

Imagine life 100 years ago. Think about what every day may have looked like for the average person. No matter where in the world you are imagining, hopefully, you picture things as they were: undeniably harder.

In 1922, the world was in a constant state of danger. Without the conveniences of modern technology, the usual daily chores—most of which fell on the shoulders of women—took ten times longer. Vaccines were rarer and hard to come by. Regardless of how much we may look back fondly on the fashion, music, or atmosphere of the twenties, it was far from a safe, calm time.

Now think back another 100 years: 1822. Life was, an even more, dangerous place! Every major city was crowded to the point that disease spread like wildfire, and to make matters worse, germ theory had yet to be accepted. Most "medicine" was little more than herbal tea or instructions to "take time by the sea." The average life expectancy was only around 40 years, largely driven by the massive number of child deaths.

No matter how far you look back, the same pattern arises again and again. No matter how difficult things may feel socially, life only gets safer with every generation.

Why, then, have rates of anxiety never been higher?

Though we live in an undeniably safe time—lower rates of crime than at nearly any point in history—we also live in a world of constant stimuli. All around us, bright lights, loud noises, and constant activity bombard our minds. 100 years ago, these would all have been seen as signs of danger; now, they are just life as usual.

Be honest: when is the last time you went a full twelve hours without looking at a screen?

Whether we are surfing the web, checking Facebook, or getting work done, we are flooding our minds with all the signals that it was once trained to process as "warning signs." Because the mind of a mother is even more attuned to the hidden signs of danger, it is even more easily overwhelmed by this constant information.

Even if you do not actively feel tired, your mind may be exhausted from the constant rush. An exhausted mind is an anxious one.

The next time you find yourself subconsciously gritting your teeth, consider what this is doing to your motherly instinct. Take a beat and remember to care for yourself. In doing so, you are actively nurturing that all-powerful bond with your daughter.

Now, let's move on to the next issue that might be affecting your motherly instinct: emotional absorption.

For most people, it's natural to slightly take on the emotions of those around us. When you see a crying child, for example, it's natural to feel a little pinch of sadness in your own heart as well. At its core, this is typically a good thing! This manner of empathy makes the world a better place, helping us all to feel more attuned to the feelings of those around us.

Research shows that mothers have an even more heightened sense of this empathy, especially when it comes to their own children. In other words, when your daughter is in pain, so are you!

In one study, researchers placed a group of babies in a room with their mothers. As the mothers sat, played, and interacted with their smiling babies, the scientists recorded the babies' facial expressions. Then, they requested that the mothers leave the room. As the mothers turned their backs and walked away, these researchers again recorded the babies' responses to being on their own.

In a separate room, these researchers placed MRI scanners on each woman, then replayed the two recordings. The results were astounding!

Whenever each woman heard her baby laughing, her mind responded with a flood of joy, mirroring that of her child. When it came to the tapes of the babies crying, the results were even more extreme. As one might expect, each woman felt a certain level of distress on hearing or seeing any child upset. Whenever her own child began crying, however, the areas of her own mind sensing danger lit up like a Christmas tree! Mentally, she felt similar levels of distress as her child, and she was mentally prepared to take whatever action she could to stop it.

All this, even as she knew that there was no real danger present.

What this research shows is that as a mother, your instinct leads you to mirror the emotions of your child.

Now, take a moment to think back to your youth. Remember being a teenage girl? How, no matter the day, your feelings always seemed to fall to extremes? Remember how a bad day always struck your heart like the end of the world, how a great day resonated in your mind as euphoria?

Imagine feeling all that now, without any understanding of the source.

Just by looking at your daughter, you somehow absorb some of her underlying emotions. When she is distressed, you may feel as if you are physically in pain. When she laughs, you might feel as if you would pull the moon down from the sky just to keep her happy.

While all this is a beautiful, natural thing, it can also be a problem if you don't take time to consider the negative effects. Right now, your daughter is experiencing more emotions than she likely ever will at any other point in her life. As her body pumps out new, changing hormones every day, she battles with exhaustion, irritability, and wild mood swings. By taking these on for yourself, you may accidentally be making the issue even more difficult.

Whenever tempers flare, take a moment to assess why you are feeling the way that you are. Are your emotions being heightened by your daughter's own stress? If this is the case, separate yourself from the situation, take a breath, and remind yourself that patience and respect are the only true ways to begin healing this amazing connection.

Modeling Respect

When emotions are heightened—whether this is by hormones or overwhelmed instincts—it's easy for tempers to flare. After all, consider all the things that you take on during the average day: work, chores, arranging for dinner, carrying your kids to all their activities, and the pressure of being the one person everyone in the family turns to for their needs. It's really a miracle you've had it together as long as you have! Still, though your exhaustion or impatience is completely understandable, they can be counterproductive to your overall goal of bonding with your daughter.

As I mentioned before, teenagers can be a pain.

They can be moody, angry, and difficult to understand. They may leave you feeling as if you want to pull your hair out. The way they occasionally act, you may feel as if you have never experienced a more disrespectful creature.

This all aside, it's vital that if you want to receive respect from your daughter, you must first model it.

When struggling to show patience and respect in the face of your daughter's moodiness, try repeating the following mantra: Be patient, be honest, and be kind.

It's been said that "patience" is one of the very highest virtues. After 25 years of helping mothers reconnect with their daughters, I can tell you with certainty that this is a fact! As hard as it can be sometimes, it's vital to remember that, above all, you are the adult in your relationship. Whenever the two of you are fighting, you are still the one with the upper hand. You come to the table with the benefit of time, the benefit of experience. She comes with nothing more than her uncontrolled emotions, limited perspective, and all the stress of teenage angst.

If one person in this situation is going to have to maintain their patience, it is going to have to be you.

As hard as it can be sometimes, true, open honesty can go miles in helping you repair your strained relationship with your daughter. At this point in her life, she is in the process of learning more adult truths, and if you are not the one who she feels she can turn to with her questions, she may try looking in less reliable places. It is important that after a fight with a friend, questions about a crush, or a moral issue, she feels as if you are a safe place.

In creating an atmosphere where your daughter knows she can come to you for an honest, unjudgmental answer, you are sending her a valuable message: you see her for the adult she is becoming.

Of every portion of the mantra, this one can be the most difficult. After all, how do you start a pattern of honest communication if every interaction with your daughter feels like a fight?

Start with the little things: tell her when you are having a bad day. Tell her why. It's okay to leave out the tiny, complicated details—she is still a child, after all, and you don't want to emotionally dump your problems onto her—but tell her that you are feeling stressed. Then, model how to safely adapt to that stress.

Right now, your daughter is likely overwhelmed with her own influx of emotions, but unlike you, she does not have experience in labeling them. By telling her in calm, quiet tones about your own feelings, you are helping her learn to better control her own. You are also setting a standard that tells her that you are a human, and you respect that she is human as well.

Finally, above all, always remember to be kind.

Kindness can mean any number of things: fixing someone their favorite meal, complimenting their appearance, asking about their day. Even in the little ways, we show kindness by maintaining eye contact or practicing active listening skills.

Unfortunately, it is easy to fall into the trap of showing more kindness to strangers than we do the people we see every day. The next time your daughter is angry, upset, or combative, think of ways you can actively show her kindness despite this. Leave a note on her mirror for her to see the next day as she's getting ready, reminding her that she's beautiful as she is. Tell her you listened to that song she's been playing, and you love the beat of it. Pick up her favorite candy bar as a surprise to find in her bookbag later.

Will she roll her eyes at your attempts? Absolutely! Will they be worth the effort regardless? Without a doubt.

In Summary

Before you can take steps towards healing your relationship with your daughter, you must understand the emotions that have led to its collapse in the first place.

Everything we think and feel is shaped by our experience on this earth. As a mother, you have been blessed with the unique, highly complex experience of watching a special little person grow through all the stages of life. You got the pleasure of watching her grow from a curious, loving toddler into the independent, strong-willed young woman who stands before you today. It is okay to mourn the loss of that precious, sweet-faced baby, but don't do so at the risk of missing out on the person your daughter is becoming.

As a mother, you get the pleasure of experiencing a set of heightened instincts and an amazing, soul-level bond with your daughter. In addition to giving you the tools you need to sense her needs, they can also allow you to incidentally absorb her own angst. This gift can quickly turn into a curse unless you remind yourself to nurture the healthy side of your motherly instinct rather than the unhealthy habits.

Lastly, remember that the best way to earn respect is to model what that looks like to you. Remember that, even in the middle of her worst, nastiest behavior, your daughter is ultimately not the adult in the relationship. She is still learning, and it is up to you as her mother to help her on that journey.

Mistakes happen; no one is perfect. Whenever you have a bad day or lose your temper, don't be too hard on yourself. You're only human, after all! Apologize, let go of the past, and move on to the healthy relationship you have been longing for.

Application Workbook 1

In the meantime, try a few of these easy action steps. By putting these activities into practice, you are putting in the work required to nurture this relationship with your daughter into one you both equally cherish:

- **Create a scrapbook of your favorite memories throughout your daughter's childhood**, then ask her to look over them with you. If she refuses, leave this scrapbook by her door, along with one of her favorite childhood treats.
- Whenever you find yourself reminiscing about years gone by, stop and **acknowledge five things you love about who your daughter is becoming**.
- **Take time for yourself.** One evening per week, put away your phone, turn off the television, and actively practice self-care. If she is open to it, ask your daughter to join you in this reduced screen time.
- When your emotions are building, **repeat your mantra:** be patient, be honest, and be kind.
- Practice honesty. **Share both one good thing and one bad thing** that happened in your day and encourage your daughter to do the same. The specific instructions take the pressure off of her to open up about her entire mental state.
- **Make a list of ten things** you can do to show active kindness to your daughter this week.

Step 2: Understanding Your Daughter

Take a moment to think about the biggest, reoccurring arguments you have ever had with your daughter.

What was it about?

How did it start?

How did it finish?

Chances are when you take a moment to step back and look at the argument objectively—really look at it—you may realize that the subject matter was not actually that important in the first place. In fact, you may find that what at that moment felt like the most earth-shatteringly important thing at that moment is no more than a trivial annoyance in the cold light of day. Once tempers flare, it is easy for even you, with your years of experience and patience, to turn a molehill into a mountain.

Is it any wonder, then, that your daughter was unable to keep her calm?

Though teenagers can often be real jerks, there is a good reason for this. As their minds and bodies are flooding with a changing mix of hormones, they are in a kind of battle. Every emotion is charged to another level, leaving them feeling as if they are drowning in a sea of misunderstanding. Later, they will be able to look back on this time in their lives and laugh, but now, at this moment, all they can see is their own highly specific, highly charged perspective.

Take Sarah, for instance. If she were to recount the previous day's argument, shaped entirely by the mold of her teenage perspective, that story would go very differently.

Through her Eyes

Sarah dragged her feet through the door, so exhausted she felt as if her shoes were weighed down with lead. The school day only lasted around eight hours, but the constant rush made her feel as if it had been weeks since she'd first left the house. All day, she'd been subject to criticism from everyone around her. The teachers spoke to her as if she was a child, rushing her from one class to another and flying into a full rage if she was late. Most days, she went as long as four full hours without going to the bathroom, too afraid of what might happen if she missed the tardy bell.

Lunch wasn't much better. The portions were so small, and by the end of the fourth block, she was so hungry that she felt she could die. She spent the entire class willing her stomach not to growl. Coach McArthur was one of those who thought it was funny to point that kind of thing out, and Sarah was already in a state of near embarrassment in that class. This was the one class a day she shared with Jake, the boy she had been crushing on since sixth grade.

Which was another problem.

Today, she and Jake had been paired together on a project. At first, her stomach flipped at this news. She cursed herself for having slept in this morning—honestly, how important was sleep, anyway? —and made a vow that tomorrow she would actually fix her hair. She had tried to act cool, but every word out of her mouth just made her feel stupider than the last. If he had ever had anything resembling a crush on her, it was sure to be over now.

Spending the last quarter of her day on high alert left her feeling even more exhausted and starving than usual. She walked straight to the kitchen and had to stop herself from dipping her fingers directly into the jar of peanut butter. Too many calories. Sarah reminded herself that she was only a few weeks away from Spring break, a season of bathing suits and tanning, and forced herself to put the jar back.

Just then her mom walked into the room.

"How was your day?"

"Fine," Sarah answered, distracted. Mentally, she was doing the math on the macronutrients in her lunch, trying to figure out if she deserved to eat a snack. Her mother said something else to her, but Sarah didn't really hear her until she started screaming.

The minute she sensed her mother's tone, Sarah had to fight the urge to curse. She told her that she would clean whatever mess she was yelling about in a minute. Just then, the dog ran in, and Sarah's stomach dropped to her shoes as she realized: she'd left the door open again.

At first, she thought her mom might not notice, but when their eyes locked, Sarah understood that they were in for another uncomfortable night.

Later, when she was crying in her room, all Sarah could think about was how unfair it all was. She knew she was not a bad kid.

She knew it!

She never snuck out, caused a problem in school, drank, or did any of the other things that the kids her age so often laughed about in class. Just last week, a girl had cussed out the teacher when she tried to pick up her cell phone in class. Sarah would never!

Most of the time, she felt as if she were barely making it from one moment to the next, and there was her mother right in her way, criticizing her every step of the way. Expecting her to be perfect. Expecting her to be like her older sister.

Her mother did not understand her or the pressure she was under. Things had been so different when she was young. There hadn't been social media, telling you that you have a responsibility to document all the fun you're having, telling you to be pretty and funny and cool all the time. She didn't understand how exhausting it was to spend eight hours sitting in a classroom, then rush off to your soccer game, then still have homework to complete when you rolled back in the door at 8 p.m. Sarah's mom complained about her nine to five job; Sarah would like to see her take on one of her thirteen-hour days!

Sometimes, the pressure of it all made Sarah just wish she could just run away.

Adolescence

For someone living with a teenager, it can be easy to laugh at Sarah's frustrations. After all, how important is a thirteen-year-old's crush in the grand scheme of things? How many adults would love a chance to go back to this phase of life, when their biggest worries were all focused on that week's soccer game?

Though there is certainly a bit of melodrama related to Sarah's emotions, pointing this out would be more than just cruel. It could be detrimental to her long-term development.

Much of Sarah's frustration comes from her current phase of life: adolescence.

As the stage between true childhood and adulthood, adolescence can be a confusing time, to say the least. Serving as a type of "in-between" phase, it operates in order to help children better develop their own understanding of themselves and their place in the world. One of the final and most important stages of your child's development, adolescence comes in three distinct phases.

Between the ages of ten and thirteen, children exist in a state of early adolescence. At this phase, they are undergoing rapid emotional, mental, and physical changes, all of which set the scene for what most parents know as the "true teenage years."

Remember Sarah coming home so ravenous she could barely think? That was for good reason. In early adolescence, children's bodies are in a state of rapid growth. As the boys grow taller and begin to experience deeper voices, the girls begin to fill out. Their hips and legs take a different shape as they begin to look less like children and more like the young women they are becoming. For many girls, this change can introduce insecurities they may have never felt before. Like Sarah, they begin to worry about their appearances and how they look to the world around them. For the first time, they might start to hear their peers talk about "counting calories" and learn that being at home in their bodies is something that they took too easily for granted.

At this point, young teens and tweens are likely to only think in terms of black and white. Though they are on their way to becoming true adults, they are not yet capable of the kind of advanced thinking that allows them to picture a situation from different perspectives. When Sarah senses that tone from her mother, she does not stop to think about why. She only feels a deep sense of injustice. In her truest of hearts, she feels as if she has been wronged.

And what is Sarah's response to being wronged? Running to the shelter of her bedroom.

At this phase of adolescence, children are likely to value their privacy above all else. They need their alone time to reconsider elements of their day, be alone with their thoughts, and feel safe. Most importantly, having their own space allows them to feel a sense of control at a time when all else may feel completely out of their hands.

As a thirteen-year-old, Sarah is right at the cusp of that next, most important stage: middle adolescence.

Lasting from age fourteen to seventeen, middle adolescence is when children undergo the most drastic mental changes, many of which involve their romantic aspirations.

As Sarah is just beginning to experience, this is a phase when "schoolyard crushes" begin to turn into something far more serious. As if by the flip of a switch, teens start to really pay attention to who catches their eye. While they likely experimented with the idea of "dating" in elementary school, that was something more similar to having a friend who let you hold their hand. Now, crushes become all-consuming, taking up all their thoughts and energy.

At this phase of adolescence, teens may be better equipped to see the "gray areas" of life, but they still struggle with the idea of true right and wrong as they fight their way toward independence. Just like in early adolescence, this often leads to arguments and fights as the teenager comes to terms with the reality of life and learns that not every question has a clear answer.

By the time teenagers enter late adolescence at the age of eighteen, all these battles finally wind their way down to an end. Just as their physical development comes to an end, so does much of their emotional instability. Finally, friendships are capable of maintaining a healthy balance. Romantic relationships are no longer all-consuming, as teenagers learn to balance their own personal interests with those of their partners. Ideally, they are in the process of learning who they want to be, just in time to make vital career and educational decisions. Though this stage of adolescence can be fraught with its own stress, their new life perspectives give teens the tools they need to handle that stress with more ease, grace, and forgiveness.

At any age, adolescence can be a roller coaster. It's natural that, as a parent, you feel an urge to protect your child from all the heartbreak and mood swings this can include. However, as much as it can hurt, every ounce of this time—hardship included—is incredibly important to your child's development. The best thing you can do is sit down, strap in, and get ready for the ride!

Brain Development

In the midst of all this change, it can be helpful to gain a solid understanding of what exactly is happening to your teen's brain development throughout these years.

Imagine your child as a kind of house. As the years pass, they undergo expansions, building on both their physical size and own complexity. They add new rooms, grow to new levels, and in the end, barely resemble the tiny structure you first knew them as.

However, though they have grown, most of the interior is still the same. The décor is similar enough that you know this home to be the one you first felt such comfort in all those years ago. The home is bigger but in no way strange or unfamiliar. In fact, much of the space here is filled with things you placed there yourself! All the ideas were yours. As you look around this house, you can see your fingerprints everywhere and know, for sure, that you were the main inspiration behind much of what you see.

Then the teenage years come along, and your child begins to remodel.

The brain development that your child experiences for much of this stage of life are like a "remodel" to their own mind. Up until now, much of what they felt, thought and believed came directly from you. Now, in the face of their journey to discover who they really are, their thoughts begin to break apart, reassemble, and form again into something entirely new.

As a parent it can be scary to watch—have you seen some of the styles these kids come up with? —but be patient. This is all a natural part of the process.
Their thoughts and feelings are not the only things to change. So does the physical makeup of the brain itself.

At this point in development, the teen's brain begins to shed unused matter and better focus its development on the parts that matter. The "gray matter," or unused connections, literally fall away as the brain changes to become something better suited to help your child function in the real world.

This change begins at the very back of the brain, moving forward slowly. The last part of the brain to experience this remodel is near the front, an area known as the prefrontal cortex (Brain development in pre-teens and teenagers. Raising Children Network).

As an unfortunate trick of science, the prefrontal cortex is the portion of the brain most active during decision-making. This is the part of the mind that gives someone the ability to think critically when making important life choices: whether to marry that guy in the band or get a degree in basket weaving. This is the portion of the brain that controls impulses, preventing us all from making the hundreds of bad decisions we would if there was not that nagging little voice telling us to slow down.

Ever seen that Disney movie *Pinocchio,* with the little cricket who follows Pinocchio around and tries to stop him from making all the wrong choices? That's what the prefrontal cortex does in real life, and in most cases, it does not actually form until our mid-twenties.
In the absence of a fully formed prefrontal cortex, the amygdala—otherwise known as the portion of the brain handling emotions—steps in to pick up the slack.

This is the equivalent of having a raging bull as your conscience. While it's better than nothing, it is far from the best option.

The next time you feel your teenage daughter becoming overly aggressive, don't waste time wondering if you're being overly sensitive or making it all up in your head. You aren't crazy.

At the same time, avoid falling into the trap of blaming your daughter for her emotions. When she handles unfortunate conflict with tears or anger, she is not being dramatic for effect. She is only doing the best she can with the tools her brain has given her. Be patient and kind with her during this time, and understand that, as long as you maintain a respectful environment, things will get better with time.

Emotions and Mental Health

Every person on Earth—from the most reasonable person you know to the most "dramatic"—deals with the ups and downs that come from occasional mood swings. For most of us, they are a small part of life. For many teenagers, it can be a daily occurrence.

Take a moment to consider the last time you were faced with a terrible case of "road rage." Zoom back to that exact moment and try to remember as many details as possible. When that complete jerk cut you off in traffic, what thoughts poured into your head? How did you feel? Think about the pressure that mounted in your chest, the way you felt as if you could have just gone off on that other driver in a hundred different foul-mouthed ways.

In that moment, what would you have said if the person in the passenger's seat told you that you were being "dramatic?"

Life with a teenager—especially a teenage girl—can occasionally feel as if you are trapped in a house with someone who has a perpetual case of road rage. Though this can be far from easy to deal with, telling your daughter to "just calm down" or trying to convince her that her feelings are not worth the effort is just a waste of time. No matter how silly the source of her attitude seems, the emotions she is feeling are entirely real.

What's more, these wild mood swings are not her fault! They are the fault of her still-developing brain chemistry, which ignored her reasonable prefrontal cortex and allowed her aggressive amygdala behind the wheel instead.

Unfortunately, this phase of life takes an enormous amount of patience. Whenever you see your daughter caught up in a swing of emotion, don't try to downplay their importance. Instead, sit with her in them.

If your daughter is crying over a friend who you always knew was no good, don't remind her that she's only known this girl a year, and never say "I told you so!" Instead, tell her that you are sorry for her hurt. Tell her that sometimes, life is hard, and when that happens, it is okay to feel sad about it.

Whenever your daughter gets an attitude simply because you asked her for help around the house, resist the urge to remind her of all you've done for her. It won't do an ounce of good, not while she's caught up in the teenage version of "road rage." Instead, give her space, and tell her that you will calmly revisit the conversation later, once she has had a chance to cool down.

Mood swings are normal. They are a natural part of life and a vital part of growing up. As annoying as they can be to deal with as a parent, these ups and downs are important steps for your daughter as she investigates her own mind and learns more about who she is as a person.

What do you do whenever these mood swings are more than a simple annoyance, though? How can you tell when they are the source of something much deeper, much more problematic?

Sadly, our country is in the middle of dealing with a major mental health crisis, and teenagers are at high risk of falling into the muck. According to research from the World Health Organization, one out of every seven teenagers deal with a major mental health problem, which, if left untreated, can be detrimental to their long-term success.

Adolescence is hard enough as it is; dealing with these difficult years while also facing a mental health problem can feel suffocating and unbearable. Teenagers struggling with mental health issues are far more likely to face social exclusion and educational issues, leading to severe problems at school or work. Furthermore, they are likely to seek out risky behavior, like drug experimentation or unsafe sex.

Of all the mental health issues that commonly plague teenagers, the worst by far are anxiety and depression. Though both conditions are entirely separate and distinctive, they include many of the same outward signs: lack of energy, disinterest in hanging out with friends, mood changes, poor health, lower test scores, and stranger sleeping patterns.

If you worry that your child may be suffering from anxiety or depression, do not be afraid to speak out about it. Though mental health issues once faced major stigma in our country, thankfully, this generation is turning that tide. While in our youth, the idea of speaking out about your feelings was wrapped in layers of shame, the generation of our children has grown into a more open, accepting society. Chances are that your daughter will have far less problem opening up about these issues than you might imagine. Just be sure that this conversation is held in a neutral, accepting way. Rather than confronting the topic when emotions are high, wait until she is experiencing one of her "ups" rather than struggling with a "down."

Outside of these mental health conditions, there is one other that has been known to plague teenagers throughout history: eating disorders.

While many believe that eating disorders are born of poor self-esteem, this is often not the case. Eating disorders most often appear in the teenage years as a way for young people to gain control in situations that leave them feeling helpless. In a world where they feel as if no one understands their problems and simply bosses them around, controlling their food intake becomes a way to self-soothe (World Health Organization).

Unfortunately, once this disordered eating takes hold, it can be a difficult pattern to break. To dissuade this pattern of eating, try and make food a focus of positive time for the family. Be open about healthy eating habits, especially when paired with exercise.

More importantly, be the model you want your daughter to follow.

Be honest: how often does your daughter hear you talk negatively about your appearance? Do you ever spend time after lunch logging your calories rather than asking about her day? During swimsuit season, do you negatively comment on your stomach, and your thighs?

Remember, your daughter is a sponge; she sees everything you do, and she soaks it up.

Before you can take steps to repair your daughter's self-image, you should first turn that same lens on yourself. The number one way you can support your daughter's mental wellness and self-confidence is by providing her the example she so desperately needs of a strong, healthy woman.

Her Priorities

There exists a mindset that says all teenagers are frivolous, that they live in a fog of apathy, not caring about anything at all. Or else, people speak of teenagers as if the things they care about are unimportant.

In truth, both thoughts could not be further from the truth.

In reality, teenagers care, almost to a point of harm!

They care about school. They care about impressing their peers. They care about pleasing their parents and teachers. They care about their appearance. They care about their style. They care about their health. They care about the health of those around them.

The list goes on and on.

Their minds are crowded with an influx of priorities, and they often feel fatigued at the idea of learning how to begin caring for all these things at once. Feeling as if they are downing in concerns, they may find it easier just to put everything on the back burner, happier to fail at all their worries than let any one person down.

All too often, when a parent sees their child neglecting important areas in their life, they deem them "lazy." What is the age-old fix for a lazy child? Teach them responsibility.

The problem with this approach comes when the source of your daughter's lack of energy isn't laziness at all, but emotional exhaustion. In this case, the opposite approach may be exactly what the doctor ordered.

Rather than piling further responsibilities onto your already overwhelmed child, have a conversation about where her efforts are better spent. For example, tell her which parts of her life you consider more important, and listen when she explains her view.

Is she exhausted from trying to balance both her nightly math homework and her travel-league soccer team? It might be time to either cut out a practice per week or be ready to accept a "B" rather than an "A."

Is she worried that she is being left out of her social circle because they are all part of a club that she no longer has time for? Maybe budget one weekend per month fully dedicated to a slumber party/pizza night, just to help her feel connected with her peers.

Rather than having the same fight about her inability to keep her bathroom clean every week, try giving her a small task that must be completed every day: wash the dishes, make her bed, or sweep the living room.

By reducing her tasks into smaller items with a clear beginning and end, you make it easier for her to learn to set her own goals. Once your daughter has a better idea of how she wants to prioritize different elements of her life, she will no longer feel the same pressure. Help her make an active decision about her priorities and watch her flourish in the face of this newfound control she feels over her life.

Regardless of your ultimate decision, one thing stands true.

This result must be one you reach together.

In Summary

At the end of the day, it is important to remember that, though she may not like hearing this, your daughter is just a kid.

Though her perspective may be deeply swayed by the intensity of her emotions, that does not make her point of view any less important than your own. Just as every person sees the world through the lens of their experience, your daughter is only capable of seeing life through her own. In her story, she is often the misunderstood hero, while the adults in her life are holding her back from the things she wants.

As tough as this can be to handle, the only thing you can do is maintain patience and understanding.

Adolescence is a strange time, as children are quickly encountering a rush of physical and mental milestones. All this change can be disorienting, leaving them feeling as if they have a lack of control over their own lives. Of all the disorienting changes, none can be more difficult to handle than the changes occurring within their own brain chemistry.

As teenagers transition from childhood to adulthood, their minds transition as well. Old, unused connections are shed to make way for new neural activity. This complicated process moves from the back of the brain to the front, meaning that for many years, the prefrontal cortex is left unformed. This important area of the brain typically controls decision-making and impulse control, and without it, teenagers often seem moody or emotional.

As a parent, it's important to remain patient with your daughter throughout this time in her life. Though there is typically no excuse for disrespectful behavior, for some time, your daughter may actually have one!

Always remember: as difficult as this phase of life is for you, it is doubly so for her. Model the behavior you want her to show, set firm boundaries, and be consistent in making sure those boundaries are followed. Stay the course, and make sure to care for yourself along the way. There may still be a few rough years ahead!

Application Workbook 2

As you wait for these difficult years to pass, don't forget to be grateful for all the beauty they bring. Your daughter is growing from a child into a woman; celebrate that! To help you celebrate this and bond with your daughter in the process, try a few more action steps:

- After a fight, **write a letter describing your perspective** of the event to your daughter. Be sure to use calm, neutral language that won't leave her feeling as if you are pointing blame. Rather than

saying "you did..." phrase things with the emphasis on yourself, saying "When this happened, I felt..."
- **Ask your daughter to write her own letter** about the situation.
- Celebrate her growing adolescence with a **"remember when" day.** Take her to all her favorite childhood locations for old favorite treats, reminisce on her best times there, and **inquire about what makes her happy now**.
- To encourage more of your daughter's "ups," ask if there is any new skill she has been wanting to learn. **Remove one of her responsibilities** as long as she commits to learning this skill. **Sign her up for a class, help her practice, and encourage her new interest! Learn a healthy new recipe** and ask your daughter to cook it with you. As she does, take the time to focus on the health rather than the calories of the meal.

Step 3: Her Circle of Influence

Remember being a teenager? That feeling of freedom, that lack of responsibility. Remember the joy of being in high school, the rush of that first intense crush, the closeness you felt with all your best friends?

Take all those memories, put them aside, and remind yourself of the truth: those memories are not reality.

Our minds have a talent for glossing over the worst of the past and glorifying the highlights. We choose to omit the worst parts of our teenage years—the heartbreak, the betrayal, the constant desire for freedom that we never seem to get—and place an overinflated sense of value on the best aspects. It's easy to only remember the pep rallies when your mind wants to forget the heartbreak of not being invited to the game itself.

Are the stresses we face in adult life have more significant weight than those we experienced during our teenage years? Absolutely. Does that mean that those years were all sunshine and rainbows? Absolutely not.

By forgetting all the hardships that come hand-in-hand with the teenage experience, parents slowly build a wall between themselves and their daughters. Every flippant statement is just another brick, adding to the difficulties they face in communication later.

Just because you aren't talking to your daughter doesn't mean that she's being closed-lipped. It's all too likely that, without you as a safe, non-judgmental space, her circle of influence is simply changing to one that is less likely to truly benefit her emotional well-being.

In this chapter, we will be discussing the pain points your daughter may be facing behind the scenes, as well as how to grow your own positive influence in her life.

But first, let's return to Sarah and Carol.

Her Circle

A few days after their last big blow-up, Carol and Sarah's relationship still felt frayed at the edges. Carol walked on eggshells around her daughter, afraid of triggering another episode. In turn, Sarah was even quieter than usual, more withdrawn than ever.
However, after what felt like ages, the cold front began to pass. There was finally a change in the air. After a seemingly endless period of tense dinners and quiet evenings, Carol finally took action. Rather than waiting for their relationship to get better or for her daughter to grow up, Carol decided to take an active role in repairing their relationship. Late at night, she scrolled through parenting blogs, searching for solace from other mothers like herself. She poured through parenting literature and took notes on ways she could help her daughter feel loved and

appreciated. She researched the psychology of the teenage mind and placed herself in Sarah's shoes, forcing herself to ignore her positive recollections of her teenage years and reframe her expectations. Finally, she made contact with a relationship expert, someone whose years of experience she hoped could help her better learn what was causing this shift in her daughter's behavior.

On the advice of this expert, Carol took off work early and picked Sarah up from school for a surprise afternoon off. She was sad to note that, when Sarah first stepped into the car, she looked more suspicious than pleased with the surprise.

"What's going on?" she said, "Has someone died or something?"

Carol laughed at the joke even though she didn't find it funny. "No, I just thought you and I could maybe go grab some ice cream. Soccer practice was canceled, and I had the afternoon free, so why not?"

After a moment's hesitation, Sarah nodded and then buckled her seatbelt.

As they drive in silence, Carol had to fight an urge to pepper her daughter with questions. Sarah's eyes looked even more tired than usual, which is saying something because she's spent the last two evenings locked in her room. Carol saw from Sarah's online grade book that her math scores are steadily dropping. She wanted to ask her about this, but instead, she connected her Bluetooth to the car radio and handed Sarah her phone.

"You pick," she said. When Sarah looked at her in confusion, Carol continued, "you've got better music taste than I do."

Sarah scrolled through the music library, and within minutes, a screeching, angry beat thumped out of the speakers. Carol decides the soft smile on Sarah's face was worth putting up with the noise. After she scrolled through a few more songs, Sarah's shoulders seemed to loosen up as she shook along with the latest pop hits. Carol pretended to enjoy them. Finally, she risked asking one of the dozen questions that's been on her mind.

"So, who showed you this artist? Was it Bella?"

Sarah's eyes turned dark for a moment, but she answered anyway. Carol takes that as a good sign.

"I don't know," Sarah says. She paused for a long time, but Carol didn't interrupt. Finally, Sarah added, "I don't really talk to Bella much anymore."

"Really? Why is that?"

"I don't know... She and Charlotte got super close over the summer, and now they don't invite me to stuff as much anymore. Like, we still talk at lunch sometimes, but I see on Snapchat that they hang out, like, every weekend."

At the idea of her baby being pushed out of this childhood friend group, Carol was seeing red. "Are they being mean to you?"

Sarah shook her head and stared out the window. "No, it's not like they're rude or anything. They never talk about it when I'm around, but that honestly just makes it weirder. It's like they don't want to rub it in my face or something. It's like they feel sorry for me."

Carol took a breath, remembering the importance of not letting her own stress show in her face and voice. Once she was sure that she was in a calm frame of mind, she added, "I'm so sorry you're going through that. Friend breakups are tough for sure. When I was your age, I honestly felt way worst after breaking up with a friend than I did about breaking up with a boy. Do you want to talk about it?"

"No, I think I'm good." For the first time in days, Sarah smiled at her, and Carol felt as if the sun was shining in her heart. It wasn't a big smile and didn't last long, but Carol was grateful for it nonetheless.

After a moment, Sarah said, "I'm excited about a chill afternoon together."

Though it is incredibly sad, what Sarah was experiencing is all too common at this age. During the teenage years, as children's personalities grow and mature, their friend groups change many times over. In many cases, this is a happy change, as children naturally gravitate towards others who better engage in their interests, but this does not make the transition any less painful. The process of letting go of the past and embracing future bonds is a difficult one, even for many experienced adults. In the mind of a growing child, it can feel immensely overwrought with heartbreak and stress.

According to research from neuroscientist Dylan Gee of Yale University, while mothers are perfectly adapted to help combat the stress many children undergo throughout childhood, they are less skilled at navigating the stressors associated with the years following puberty (Swamy). Often, this is because much of this stress comes from deeper emotions, feelings of isolation, and a need for understanding. When children feel as if they cannot turn to their parents for these needs, they instinctively form fast, close friendships to fill in that vital emotional gap. For a mother, the transition can be jarring. One moment, you feel as if your baby trusts you with everything, and the next, they turn exclusively to friends. As these friend groups undergo major changes, it can feel even more impossible to know who your daughter is trusting with her most prevalent emotions.

Luckily, after Carol's research, she understood these feelings and knew the steps to take in navigating them.

Rather than dumping her own emotions on her daughter or making her feel guilty for leaving out this information about her changing friendships, Carol empathized. She let her know that, even if she did not perfectly understand Sarah's situation, she did not feel that her daughter was dramatic in experiencing feelings of sadness. Rather than saying, "this is just what happens as you get older," she said, "I remember feeling sad about something similar when I was your age." In doing so, so took a step toward dismantling the emotional wall that was built between them.

As Sarah grows and makes new, better connections, telling her mother about these new friends will feel less like a burden and more like a continuation of a conversation they have already had.

Now, Carol is in a better position to tell Sarah what she feels is the truth: unfortunately, this kind of isolation really is a part of life. Now, Sarah is in a better position to listen to that advice, welcoming her mother into that exclusive circle of influence.

Patterns and Routines

By the time Carol and Sarah reached the ice cream shop, Sarah's mood seemed considerably brightened. Though she was not quite talkative, she smiled a bit more and hadn't touched her phone since the start of the drive.

Rather than peppering her daughter with questions, Carol decided to just pass the time with mild chatting. Carol reminisced about her childhood, telling Sarah stories from days when she was in school. As she did, she tried to laugh at her hardships, hoping to demonstrate the way that most of the "downs" she felt then are only a distant memory.

Carol was deep in the memory of one of her most intense breakups when Sarah interrupted.

"Man, I wish I had time to do all that."

"What do you mean?"

Sarah shook her head and made an odd expression as she pieced together the language of her thoughts.

"I mean, it just seems like you had so much time for fun."

For the first time that afternoon, Sarah took on the bulk of the conversation, talking about how she spends her own hours. Listening to the way her daughter spoke, Carol was shocked.

Though many of the emotions of the teenage years—the heartbreak, the crushes, and the mood swings—remain the same from one generation to the next, the way these two generations spend their time has vastly changed over the years. Not only that, but the way that young men and women live their lives has undergone major transformations as well.

Recent findings from the Pew Research Center suggest that over the past several decades, teenagers' priorities have shifted dramatically, in ways that are often negative as much as they are positive.

Though this generation of teenagers is far less likely to work paid jobs than their predecessors, they somehow manage to remain just as busy. Rather than earning their own money, they instead pour their hours into schoolwork and extracurricular activities. What's more, the time spent on "leisure" is far less "leisurely" than that of previous generations.

Despite popular belief, this generation of teenagers spends far less time socializing with their peers. Instead, these hours are often eaten up with isolated screen time, with many teens spending over four hours on their phones per day (Livingston). Though some argue that, for this generation, screen time often involves a level of socialization, the facts remain that these hours spent in physical isolation miss out on many of the positive effects of time spent in the real-life company of friends and family.

To make matters worse, these studies also seem to indicate that young women are spending their time in ways that reflect a rising pressure to fit in.

With hair appointments, skincare, showers, and dressing, the average teenage girl spends over an hour per day simply on grooming routines. By contrast, young men spend around thirty or forty minutes at most. Not only that, but girls are more likely to feel more pressure to study and complete schoolwork with less time for healthy bonding activities like outdoor games or exercise.

Unfortunately, parents are often limited in what they can do about relieving this pressure for their daughters, much of which is deeply internalized.

Rather than fighting a useless fight, mothers can go a long way by working to gain an understanding of these pressures. Simply by understanding the patterns and routines that make up your daughter's hours, you can help relieve some of the intensity with which she falls victim to them.

Expressing Oneself

The afternoon ticked on, and Carol found herself losing track of time. She realized with a slight pang of guilt that this may have been the first time in weeks that she has truly enjoyed her daughter's company.

After weeks and months of slowly increasing resentment, Carol and Sarah's relationship was starting to feel less like that of a mother and daughter and more like two angry roommates. Because they spent so much time around one another, Carol took for granted the fact that she knew who her daughter was. After all, what kind of mother does not know her child?

If there was anything this afternoon is teaching her, it was that she may have known the young woman her daughter was, but she does not know that much about who she is becoming.

Before picking Sarah up from school, Carol had hoped that she might be able to slowly encourage her daughter to open up about her deepest troubles. After hours of conversation, however, the majority of the afternoon was spent talking about seemingly unimportant things: tv, movies, and music. However, something in Carol's gut—her motherly instinct—told her that this was part of what has made this afternoon so meaningful.

Though Carol had yet to put words to what she is feeling, her instinct was leading her in the right direction. For many teenagers, the process of expressing themselves in words feels like a daunting task. After all, when their minds are so often a tornado of conflicting thoughts, feelings, and emotions, how could they easily pin down exactly what they want to say? Instead, young women like Sarah often express their own emotions in the form of the media they enjoy.

Think back through your history and remember the kind of music you listened to in your teenage years. Remember how those songs used to hit you deep within your gut, making you feel as if your heart was breaking with the beauty of the words and grace of the melody? How did your own parents often respond to your passion for these songs? More importantly, how did their response make you feel?

All too often, the media that teenagers—especially teenage girls—consume is an easy target for mockery. Often, these shows and songs tend to be more experimental that what we see in the mainstream, more emotionally charged. As an adult, it's easy to make fun of the often melodramatic tone and whiny sound, but in reality, these qualities are exactly what makes the music so impactful to its young audience.

And, in the end, isn't this also what makes this art so beloved years later? Consider The Beatles, Elvis, or any number of the bands that make up our shared history. In their own day, they were often mocked for the rabid love their teenage audience felt toward them. Only in the light of time is it clear why their fans were so avidly attached: these people and groups were making some of the best music of their generations.

As Carol and Sarah sat together in that ice cream shop, the very worst thing Carol could ever do would be to tease her daughter for the art she consumes. In doing so, she would be making fun of her daughter's primary form of self-expression and making Sarah feel as if she could not truly trust her mother to take her feelings seriously.

In the end, doesn't everyone just want to feel understood?

By approaching her daughter with an element of curiosity, Carol encourages her to open up more about her music, her favorite television, her latest books, and—most importantly—herself.

Bad Influences and Bullying

After a pleasant afternoon, Carol paid for the last of their treats, and she and Sarah got in the car to head home. Carol was hoping that the act of driving would loosen Sarah up even more, and thankfully, her wish was granted.

"How's school been?" Carol asked, "Do you have any friends in any of your classes?"

"Yeah, that's all good I guess." Sarah's voice trailed off, and Carol waited patiently for her to continue. After a sigh, Sarah finally did. "I don't know. There were these girls in my English class that I would pair up with on group assignments. I thought we were friends at first, but then they just got weird."

"What do you mean, weird?"

"Like, they'd bunch up together, then stop talking when I got close enough to hear. At first, I thought it might be in my head, so I ate lunch with them a few times. It just got worse."

Inside, Carol's mind was screaming for her daughter to keep talking, but she took a breath and forced herself to stay calm. "What does 'worse' mean?" she asked.

"I don't know. I just don't think they like me very much."

The rest of the conversation felt a bit like pulling teeth as Carol gently pried the information from her daughter. On the rest of the drive home, Sarah described these two girls—who she still claimed were her friends—and told her mother about how they "accidentally" made a few comments that hurt her feelings: offhand comments about her flat chest or "stupid" laugh. They began inviting her to hang out more, but whenever she did, they seemed annoyed to have her there. Finally, just as Carol pulled up in the driveway, Sarah scrolled through her phone to reveal a set of screenshots saved in her gallery.

"The other day, Barb sent me these," she said, "They're from a group chat I did not know they had without me."

Carol gingerly took the phone from Sarah's hands and scrolled through the screenshots. They showed a text exchange about Sarah, joking about getting her to do their work for them.

"Have you been doing these girls' homework?" Carol asked, accidentally letting her voice slip into that judgmental tone she had been trying to avoid.

"Just sometimes," Sarah replied defensively, and the air in the car went icy again for a split second. Sarah sighed and said, "It's just, I've kind of been on my own a lot more lately, now that I'm not hanging out with my usual group. These girls seemed... nice. They still are sometimes." She looked up at her mother, and Carol was alarmed to see tears in her eyes. "I'm just not sure what to do."

In movies, bullies are often portrayed the same way: openly mean, snarky, and doing whatever it takes to gain power over a smaller, weaker student.

In truth, the situation is often much more complicated. Bullies work by subtly cutting down their peers over time, gaining power in small increments until the victim does not even realize how much they have given up. Often, bullies have a goal in mind, whether that is getting free work, taking another's money, or simply using the victim as a tool to feel better about their own lives.

With the rise of the internet, this bullying is often even more subtle. Rather than throwing physical punches, bullies work through their words. They use the victim's insecurities as a way to gain power over them, then reinforce those insecurities again and again.

In the case of situations like Sarah's, this back-and-forth power dynamic can complicate matters even further. Even as Sarah's bullies cut her down, they give her just enough positive attention to keep her hanging on, actively seeking their approval. Whenever she begins to feel confident enough to leave their group altogether, they turn once more, inviting her to spend time with them and making her feel special. Much like any other abusive relationship, this toxic situation is a cycle built on a series of ups and downs, leaving Sarah and hundreds of girls just like her feeling as if, were they just to hold on a little longer, they might be able to make it through the bad times and back into a truly solid foundation.

Unfortunately, there is little that Carol can do to help prevent this cycle from happening in her daughter's life. Forbidding Sarah to speak to these girls would only make her that much more adamant to befriend them if only to prove her mother wrong. Contacting the school runs the risk of embarrassing her daughter and making the problem even worse. What's more, there is very little that these girls have actually done at this point that could even warrant action on the part of the teacher! In creating harm through millions of subtle, cruel cuts rather than any large act of meanness, these girls have shielded themselves from harm. Likely, any outsider would not view this situation as anything more than teenage "drama."

However, all their tiny cruelties rely on a single, vital factor: building a repeated pattern.

Much of their power comes from the back-and-forth nature of the relationship they have built with Sarah. The pattern is everything; it's what keeps Sarah hanging on, desperate to finally earn approval she may never receive. The longer this pattern continues, the worse it will become. By breaking this pattern and denying her part in it, Sarah can put a stop to the cycle that is helping establish her bullies' power over her mood.

As a child, Sarah is not yet emotionally capable of recognizing what is happening to her. Though Carol is not in a position to make her daughter's decisions for her, she can help her recognize the early signs of a bullying relationship and give her the tools she needs to escape. Once again, this is an area in which building a foundation of open, healthy communication is vital in helping her daughter make the right decisions, separate herself from negative people and situations, and steer her toward the right path.

A great place to start is by helping connect her daughter to others who share her specific interests. Does she like theater? Even many small cities have thriving community theater programs that are always looking for young, dedicated actors. Does she hope to nurture a passion for athletics? Look for intermural teams, and as she gets older, see if she might be interested in serving as an assistant coach for younger players. When you worry your child might not be making the right social connections, don't chastise her for her poor choices. Instead, help build her confidence and connect her to activities that actually build the kind of community you hope for her future.

Attraction and Finding Love

After the momentary rough spot in the car, Carol asked Sarah if she would mind helping her with dinner. At first, Sarah declined, saying that she had to finish her homework. After a few minutes, however, she appeared in the doorway of the kitchen holding her math book in one hand and a pencil in the other. She sat at the island bar as she reviewed her algebra work, occasionally murmuring under her breath as she does.

Carol noticed the frustration on her face and asked, "Have you been having issues in math lately? I noticed that your grade is dropping in that class. Should I have a talk with Coach MacArthur?"

To her surprise, Sarah's face turned bright red. She looked away, and said, "No, it's alright."

"Are you sure? Is something distracting you?"

Sarah's already red face flushed even brighter, and she answered just a second too quickly. At that moment, Carol realized the truth.

Her daughter had a crush.

If there is one fact that remains the same across all generations, it is the intensity with which teenagers fall for that first big crush. It can feel monumental, dealing with this rush of emotion, which couldn't feel more different than the "puppy love" they are used to. Once swept away by the intensity of these feelings, teenagers often feel willing to do whatever it takes to keep that crush under wraps, nursing it like the obsession it is.

In general, teenage crushes fall into one of three categories: celebrity crushes, identity crushes, and romantic crushes.

As the name would suggest, a celebrity crush occurs when a teenager feels a rush of strong attraction towards someone famous, likely someone who they never intend on meeting. These crushes, while amusing, are often a healthy expression of their growing sexuality. As long as your daughter is capable of laughing at her own celebrity crush, there is nothing wrong with these completely natural feelings.

Identity crushes are often built on feelings of strong admiration, which the young mind confuses with true attraction. Typically, these crushes come in the form of a mild obsession with a leader or mentor, often a teacher or coach. Again, these feelings are a natural part of their growth process, and as long as they remain aware of boundaries, there is often no harm in having a slight identity crush. If anything, these crushes may function to help your daughter realize the qualities she wants to embody or obtain in her future partner.

The last category—the romantic crush—is by far the most intoxicating. While under the spell of a romantic crush, your daughter is likely to experience feelings of extreme infatuation, even bordering on obsession. She may be incapable of noticing her crush's faults, as she remains caught in the waves of fresh attraction for one of the first times in her young life. Instead, the rush of dopamine and serotonin she feels around this person inspires her to see them in only the rosiest possible light.

Though these crushes are often a safe expression of their path to maturity, they can come with a dark side. While experiencing such a strong attraction, your daughter may unknowingly shape her own behavior around that of her crush. She may change her style, slowly carving away pieces of her personality to better fit his own. Over time, she might become dependent on the rush of positive "happy" chemicals her brain feels when she is around this person, leading her to follow him around or alter her natural path to fit in with his own. In the worst cases, she might even ignore her wants and needs as she battles to keep him satiated.

This path may be one that leads your daughter to heartbreak, but unfortunately, it is a road she must travel on her own. All you can do is help her understand the early signs of a toxic situation, support her own sense of self, be sure she has a strong understanding of consent, and release her into the world to be her own person. Be sure that your daughter is aware that, regardless of how embarrassed she may be, her feelings are completely normal and a healthy part of the young woman she is on her way to becoming.

In Summary

Though life has massively changed from one generation to the next, some problems remain the same. Your teenage daughter likely struggles with the very same issues you experienced at her age—unrequited crushes, work-life balance, and the struggle to express herself—but in many ways, the manner in which she experiences these core struggles has changed. With rising awareness of empathy and the normalization of social media, bullying today looks entirely different than the bullying of our youth. Though teenagers work fewer jobs on average, the pressures they face in their schoolwork, social groups, and extracurricular activities have only grown.

Amid this sea of changes, the best step a mother can take towards helping her daughter feel understood is to first examine her own way of thinking. Rather than glorifying her teenage years, she should take a long, hard look at the emotions she truly felt during that time and educate herself on what her own daughter may be experiencing. Instead of speaking to her daughter as a child, she should approach her with a true sense of curiosity, laying down the foundation for stronger communication and opening herself up as a safe space for her daughter to turn.

Application Workbook 3

Clueless about where to start? Try putting a few of these action steps into play:

- On your own, **create a schedule** of how you imagine your daughter spends her time. Then, **have her create her own** based on her day. Compare these charts to one another and gain a better understanding of how the other fills her hours.
- **Ask your daughter to create a CD or playlist**. Listen with genuine curiosity the next time you are driving together and open the door to conversation about what draws her to all her favorite songs.
- **Plan a "romantic comedy" movie night** and take the opportunity to point out behaviors that are normal in the film but red flags in real life.

Step 4: Key Issues Today

Before we continue, take a second to think: what does "self-care" mean for the average adult?

The idea of self-care can be a minefield to navigate, as it likely looks incredibly different from one woman to the next. For some, self-care might be a night out with good friends, while others could only really decompress from the building stress through a night completely on their own, with no one asking anything of them. For those of us struggling to keep our heads above water, unfortunately, self-care often feels like the last item on any to-do list.

Regardless of how you choose to recharge after a long week, the key factor is that you likely know yourself well enough by now to know how to do so. By the time you reach this level of maturity, you understand what feeds your soul, just as you understand what pulls from your energy. Even this simple understanding can help guide you through the tough times, as you know what you can ultimately do to relax. Even if you worry you won't get that relaxing vacation or bubble bath, just the thought alone is enough to help you power through tough times.

Imagine how it would feel to be lost without any knowledge of how to self-soothe. Think about how isolating it must feel to not even know that this stress and pressure are a natural part of life.

That is likely the exact situation your teenage daughter finds herself in right now.

In the last chapter, we discussed how much of the average teenager's day is spent dealing with increasing social pressure and limited free time. In this chapter, we will discuss how increasing pressures of perfection pick away at the average teenage girl's sense of self, adding fuel to the fire of every argument and increasing her own sense of worthlessness. In the best cases, these feelings simply compile to create intense inner turmoil; in the worst, they manifest as the early signs of mental illness.

By gaining a better understanding of the pressures that your teenage daughter faces today, you can help her learn how to heal her wounds and, potentially, heal your own in the process.

Being Perfect

It's no secret that girls can be particularly hard on themselves. The intense amount of comparison they feel to others their age—whether that is induced by society, upbringing, or their own nature—can lead them to feel as if they are constantly falling behind their peers. The harder they push to "catch up," the more the competition seems to build itself up as well. It's an impossible race, one that never has a clear, definitive finish line. It has always been this way and may feel as if it's destined to be this way for the rest of time.

Though this push for perfection is a tale as old as time, that doesn't mean that it's a story locked in amber, one that will never change. Unfortunately, the research all seems to suggest that this generation of teenage girls is facing more pressure than any generation before them.

According to a recent study by the BeeWell research project, today's young women are three times as likely as young men to suffer from mental health issues related to this push for perfection (Jeffreys).

BeeWell began by surveying 40,000 teenagers, asking them how they spend their time and their emotional capacity to handle stress. The findings were astonishing. While many of the boys interviewed in this study reported feeling free to be "mischievous," hardly any girls reported feeling that same freedom to make mistakes. Around twenty-two percent of young women reported regularly feeling major emotional difficulties, while nearly half reported not being able to get enough sleep every night. Often, these overwhelmed feelings appeared related to the mounting pressures to fit in and retain the image of the perfect, desirable life.

One girl interviewed even reported dropping out of soccer—her primary outlet for feelings of sadness or aggression—after worrying how being the only girl on the team might make her look. She reported feeling pressure to maintain a certain image of femininity and success, and her role on the soccer team did not do anything to meet that image. Consequently, she mistakenly took a step away from an area that actually would have vastly improved her mental and physical health, all in the hopes of meeting that impossible standard of perfection so many teenage girls struggle to obtain.

When interviewed about how they spend their time, only around one in every five girls reported any kind of daily physical activity, even simply walking! Instead, most of this time previous generations invested in physical activity now goes into maintaining a social media presence. This action does not reflect "laziness." Rather, it showcases how these girls' limited experience in the world does not provide them with the tools they need to make healthy choices on their own. Though many girls understood the problems associated with their lack of activity, the draw of exchanging that healthy habit for an unhealthy one—scrolling mindlessly on social media, pining for the image that their peers seemed to be presenting on those platforms—was simply too tempting.

Let's be honest with ourselves: even as adults, don't we often fall into that very same trap?

As parents, we naturally want our children to become the very best versions of themselves. When we see them "messing up" and making the wrong choices, it can be easy to think it is our responsibility to whip them into shape by adding more responsibilities and punishments. Though this kind of "no-nonsense" approach to parenting can occasionally have some benefits, it can also function to add more pressure to the idea of perfection that our daughters already suffer under. It can create a standard in which they do not feel free to make the healthy mistakes that every person alive needs to experience to grow and mature.

In other words, by being too tough on our teenage daughters, we are only stifling their ability to become the happy, healthy young women we so desperately want them to be.

Lack of Motivation

How often have you argued with your daughter about any of the following: slipping grades, incomplete homework, unfinished chores, or lack of general motivation?

It's a common cycle. We see our daughters failing to complete the simple, quick tasks we have assigned them. We worry that this laziness means that they won't have the tools they need to succeed in the adult world. We become frustrated with their unwillingness to help around the house. We yell, they cry, and the horrible cycle of arguing plays once again, always on repeat in our household and making everyone around us more and more upset.

Though there is truly no easy fix when it comes to increasing your teenager's sense of motivation, there is a simple way you can put an end to this cycle of arguing: understand the science behind her struggles.

Remember the prefrontal cortex we learned about in chapter two? The part of the brain that controls decision-making and planning? This is actually the very same area of the brain that allows every adult on Earth to push through the desire to procrastinate, giving us the appearance of motivation whenever we only want to relax and ignore the outside world.

Whenever you feel that temptation to procrastinate an unwanted chore or work project, what you are experiencing is an age-old battle between two parts of your brain: the prefrontal cortex and the limbic system, which controls the pleasure centers of your brain. Though these parts of your brain are not exactly muscles, they often function similarly. Whatever part you "work out" or "feed" the most grows stronger. By spending too much time sparking up the pleasure centers of your limbic system—drinking, playing on your phone, or watching television—you only empower it to overcome that all-important prefrontal cortex more easily. The connections in that area of the mind grow weaker, only increasing the likelihood that you will struggle with procrastination again in the future (Rampton).

Believe it or not, this struggle is not always a bad thing. After all, life is all about balance. Many report that alternating between the pleasure center and the area in charge of focus and planning can actually relieve feelings of procrastination and increase levels of creativity. The key to maintaining this kind of positive balance lies in scheduled "procrastination sessions" throughout the day. Rather than trying to spread yourself over too many projects at once, focus on one at a time. Rather than filling your day with tiny, sporadic bursts of pleasure, schedule a longer break for relaxation to break up the monotony.

For our teenage daughters, whose prefrontal cortex is not fully developed, these breaks are even more vital to their growth and development.

Expecting your teenage daughter to maintain the same level of perseverance, dedication, and work ethic as a functioning adult is much like expecting an amateur weightlifter to handle the same equipment as a professional bodybuilder: pointless and disappointing. Try as she might, your daughter simply doesn't have the tools she needs to maintain a constant level of motivation. It's very likely that by the time you see her after school, her stores of energy and motivation have already been fully zapped.

In the average school day, students are expected to sit, work, and focus for eight to nine full hours, with incredibly limited breaks in between. During this time, they must remain off their phones, be silent for extended periods of time, and resist the urge to let their minds wander.

Be honest: how did you really react the last time you were expected to do the same, even just for an hour-long meeting?

This is not to say that you shouldn't hold your child to high expectations. Even if your daughter has yet to fully develop the tools she needs to learn, there is still much for her to gain from the process of regular goal-setting. Instead of increasing the pressure that she feels to meet every goal, however, try teaching her how to set appropriate breaks in the middle of her day.

During homework, restrict the amount of access she has to her phone or television. Rather than filling the day with a million tiny breaks, dictate designated time for extended relaxation. If possible, encourage her to take regular walks or increased outdoor time during busy weeks.

Most importantly, be sure that this motivation is more than just a command. For this lesson to truly stick, you have to model these same values in your own life.

Dangers of Helicopter Parenting

When you are at work, how do you feel whenever your boss micromanages you? Whenever you feel as if someone is constantly breathing down your neck, making you worry about every possible mistake, do you feel any real increase in the quality of your work? Do you feel more motivated to succeed?

Chances are that answer is "no."

The phrase "helicopter parenting" refers to the very same act between a parent and child. When a parent falls into the trap of helicopter parenting, they maintain a constant, unrelenting level of focus on their child's overall success. Often, this includes working to shield their child from any level of harm or discomfort, whereas other times, it involves an insistence that any form of "failure" is unacceptable. These parents maintain a belief in their own child's perfection.

When you look at your baby, the culmination of years of hard work and love, it can be easy to think that they are as flawless as your eyes make them feel. However, this idea can actually work against your child's long-term success, creating a system in which they no longer know how to function with a sense of failure you never let them experience.

As much as it can often hurt, failure is a part of life; nothing more, nothing less. It is how we learn, grow, and become the people we are ultimately meant to be. It's easy to think that by shielding your child from failure, you are protecting them from heartbreak, but this could not be further from the truth. By shielding your child from failure, you are only ensuring that when it inevitably happens, they are unequipped to handle the disappointment.

Whenever you worry that you may be "helicopter parenting," take a step back and ask yourself the following questions:

- Have I reminded my child of this already?
- What are the long-term consequences of this failure?
- Does she have the skills to do this on her own?
- How can I teach her the skills without completing the task?

As hard as it can be to relinquish this control, remember that they will never be able to learn until they have experienced the consequences of their own actions. By doing nothing, you are often doing the very best thing.

Self-Esteem, Anxiety, and Depression

It's not a secret; rates of anxiety and depression among teenagers have never been higher. As we discussed previously, these rates tend to be far higher in young women than in young men. These damaged emotions can make it even more difficult to connect with your daughter in times of stress or tension, as every nerve in her mind is geared toward disappointment and failure.

Though anxiety and depression are often inescapable parts of life—a nasty trick of genetics or health—they can also develop as a result of the environment. There is no magic equation for sparking these mental health disorders, but we do know what a few of the top culprits are: alcohol, nicotine, an influx of caffeine, and too much screen time. Unfortunately, these are all the vices that teenagers are most likely to turn to in times of high stress.

As teenagers develop their own ability to create and stick to long-term plans, they may experience greater struggle than the average adult. Remember, the part of your mind that helps you organize your life is being ruled by the planet of "impulsivity" in your daughter's brain! This makes it all the more likely that, whenever she encounters something that knocks her unsteady plan off balance, she is more likely to turn to easy answers that light up that pleasure center and cause a distraction.

Though it is impossible to truly protect your daughter from the effects of anxiety, low self-esteem, and depression, you can help her find the tools she needs to make healthier choices on her own. Rather than simply forbidding her to partake in that Red Bull, vape, or mindless scrolling when she is feeling overwhelmed, help her find better ways to self-soothe.

If you read any manner of parenting books when your daughter was an infant—don't worry, we've all been there—then you are likely familiar with the term "self-soothe" already. In infancy, this term often refers to the parenting strategy of allowing your child to cry on their own, teaching them to find ways to soothe their own tantrums outside of adult intervention. While there are arguments about whether or not this technique is beneficial for the baby's long-term health, nearly everyone agrees that it is a vital skill for every burgeoning young adult.

This wraps back around to the concept of self-care.

Self-care—just a fancier way of saying "self-soothing"—looks different for everyone. Just because you enjoy unwinding with a book and a bath doesn't mean it will carry the same benefits for your daughter. As her mother, you can help her find what she needs to practice healthy habits to relieve her stress without manifesting into anxiety or depression.

Listen to her during conversations. What does she seem to be jealous of in others' lives? What pictures cover her Pinterest board, Tumblr, or Instagram? When have you most noticed her being at her happiest? What are her hobbies and greatest interests?

Don't wait until you notice your daughter mid-breakdown to teach her these skills. Whenever you anticipate a season of stress, remind her of all the things she loves doing to decompress and empower her to practice those skills. If painting and coloring soothe her, treat her to a new set of pastels and an adult coloring book. For athletes, a subscription to your nearest gym may be exactly what the doctor ordered. Is your girl always watching skincare tutorials? It might be time to swing by the local Walgreens together for some face masks.

As you go through this lesson, don't forget to remind her of one vital fact: self-care is more than just fun. It also means taking care of the tedious tasks that make life more bearable in the long run. As often as self-care looks like a new facial serum, it also looks like a clean room and good hygiene. As often as it means lighting an expensive candle, it also means washing the dishes and scooping the litter box.

By teaching your child the vital skills of self-soothing, you give her the paddle she needs to direct her life through the storms it will hand her, hopefully making it easier for her to float safely to the next shore.

Mood Disorders

Unfortunately, there are some storms that no amount of bubble baths or extra sleep can cure.

Even in our mental-health-conscious world, mood disorders remain one of the most undiagnosed health problems in the nation. More intense than most cases of anxiety or depression, these disorders have the power to completely warp a person's sense of reality, changing their moods as easily as the flip of a switch. A symptom of trauma, brain chemistry, and a variety of other factors, these disorders often take years to identify.

Sadly, they appear to be most difficult to pin down in children.

This difficulty comes from a variety of different sources. One issue is that these disorders often seem to have different symptoms in children than they do in adults. Another problem is that many of the related mood swings are easily written off as hormones rather than treated as the major issues that they are. Because children are so often treated as naturally "overdramatic," they often have a harder time communicating the depth of their emotional issues, leaving the adults in their lives in the dark until it is far too late.

Children and teens suffering from mood disorders often struggle with their grades, behavior management, and relationships. They may rapidly undergo a major weight change or complain of physical aches and pains. These issues may result in problems maintaining their grades as all their focus is being poured into understanding what is happening inside their own minds. Most apparently to most parents is often the sudden swing towards highly risky and rebellious behavior.

I think it is important to take a moment to discuss what exactly qualifies as "highly risky" and "rebellious" behavior.

In my experience, I have seen where, in their fear of being left out of their daughter's changing life, mothers tend to qualify even slightly unexpected acts as rebellion. It's often easier for them to put a label on these acts rather than recognize them for what they are: normal teenage behavior. Though it may be annoying when your daughter slams the door in your face, it is not the manner of behavior I am discussing here.

Speeding on the way to school is normal; sneaking out and driving over 100 miles per hour down the interstate is dangerous.

Kissing her boyfriend is normal; secretly dating older men, acting out sexually, and devaluing her body are dangerous.

Though frustrating, it's normal for your daughter to try a beer at a local party; binge drinking to the point of belligerence is dangerous and rebellious behavior.

In nearly every case, a small amount of rebellion is actually a healthy way for your daughter to test her own boundaries and make her way in the world. When her behavior takes a turn towards true danger, however, it may be time to hire a professional to help intervene.

If you worry that your daughter's behavior may fall into the "dangerous" category rather than that of a normal teenage girl, I have one bit of advice: hire a professional. Only then can you truly be certain of how to provide your daughter with the best possible method of care moving forwards.

To provide a bit of context, I am including here a small breakdown of a few of the most common disorders to appear during the teenage years (Overview of Mood Disorders):

- Persistent depressive disorder, also known as dysthymia, is a persistent, low-grade depressive mood that continues without relief for a year or more
- Major depressive disorder involves a depressive or irritated mood that lasts for around two weeks or more
- Bipolar disorder leads to rapid variations in mood swings, often leading the teenager to experience periods of high productivity contrasted with depressive, low-energy moods
- Substance abuse mood disorder is triggered by outside abuse of drugs, exposure to toxins, or alcohol

I know how you are feeling right now: as you read the descriptions above, you feel your heart start to quicken. Your hands are itching to pull out your computer and begin googling symptoms. Resist this urge with everything you can! Furthermore, do not tell your daughter any suspicions you may have about her mental health. Though a bit of context can help decide when it might be time to call in reinforcements, you may put your daughter on the path toward failure by allowing herself to improperly identify with a disorder that she may not have.

In the end, only a professional can truly identify this manner of mental-health disorder and direct your daughter toward the proper treatment.

Substance Abuse

I would not feel safe covering this chapter's topic if I did not address one of the most problematic parts of parenting today: spotting the signs of and handling substance abuse.

Unfortunately, nearly 6,000 teens every year report experimenting with prescription pain pills alone, and thousands more branch off into a variety of other drugs from here. Once addiction has sunk its claws into a person's skin, it can prove a nearly impossible monster to shake. Though most mistakes during this period of a person's life do not have many long-term effects, developing a substance abuse disorder at this early age can go on to haunt an individual for the rest of their life.

At this stage in life, teenagers are more drawn to risk than they will possibly ever be again. To protect them from the temptations of substance abuse, be sure to restrict their access to prescription medications and other such substances. If you have a liquor cabinet, make sure it remains locked when not in use. When your daughter stays out, try and be awake when she returns to monitor her mood and sobriety. Model appropriate behavior by not regularly drinking in their presence. There is nothing wrong with cutting loose a bit on special occasions—as long as you have a designated driver, of course—but allowing your daughter to regularly see you partying or drinking could lead her to accept this as completely normal behavior.

Be aware of some of the early warning signs. Regular mood swings are natural, but wild swings that appear to spring up completely without warning might be a sign of something far more troubling. Sudden bursts of energy and talking might be related to stimulants, while "downers" lead the abuser to experience drowsiness, slurred speech, and greater difficulty with fine motor skills (Rise in prescription drug misuse and abuse impacting teens).

In addition to watching your daughter's mood, pay attention to signs of drug paraphernalia during your regular cleanup routine. This isn't always as simple as looking for a bong in your daughter's closet. Cut-up straws, empty pen cartridges, and surprisingly placed spoons can all be signs of crushing and snorting drugs. Excessive amounts of time spent in the shower may be a cover for smoking, and recurrent plumbing issues may also point to constipation that drug abusers often experience as normal life.

As a parent, it can feel like a difficult balancing act, making sure that your child is safe without allowing them to undergo this enormously risky behavior. Though it may feel impossible, parenting a growing young adult simply means accepting that this pain is part of your journey. Control what you can in your child's life, and choose to release what you know you can't control.

In Summary

Self-care is more than just a buzzword; it is a vital step in teaching your daughter the proper steps to cope with stress and avoid falling victim to depression, anxiety, and even substance abuse.

Today's young women are under more pressure than ever to fit the image of the "perfect" teenage girl. As they struggle to balance school, their social lives, their family, and the increasing pressure to have it all together on social media, they might find themselves shutting down under all the mounting stress. Though this may sometimes appear as laziness or lack of motivation, it is a symptom of poor coping skills.

Because the teenage mind is not fully formed, it is a struggle for children of this age to properly take action toward their long-term health. All too often, the allure of a "quick fix" to light up the pleasure centers of their brain feels far easier than the long, difficult task of goal setting. As a parent, you can ease this burden by modeling proper behaviors and guiding your teenager toward healthier alternatives to drugs, alcohol, nicotine, and any of the other usual vices.

Though mood swings are normal—especially in the face of all this societal pressure—in the worst situations, they may also be a sign of a deeper problem. If you fear that your daughter may be suffering from a mood disorder or substance abuse problem, it may be time to release control and take the problem to a professional.

Application Workbook 4

As you help your daughter navigate some of the key issues of her life, try bonding over a few of these action steps:

- **Watch any of the classic *Little Women* adaptations together** and take the chance to talk about the expectations of women over time. Discuss how Jo's character struggles with the norms of her society in contrast to the way your daughter struggles with her own idea of perfection.

- Work with your daughter to **schedule a weekly "phone-free evening."** Be sure to express your dedication to following through on this routine alongside her.
- Teach your daughter the value of organized self-care by **giving her one weekly/daily task to help her learn the value of caring for her environment**. This can be as simple as washing her hair, making her bed, or picking her clothes up off the floor.
- In exchange for following through on this chore, **take your daughter to Walmart and give her a budget for monthly self-care needs.** This can be as big or small as you'd like, depending on your family's budget.
- **Have an open and frank discussion about the dangers of substance abuse.** Share with her any concerns you may have, using a neutral tone of voice to avoid showing judgment.

Step 5: Connection

In the earlier chapters of this book, we focused on the all-important task of understanding your daughter, building patience, and knowing what is truly going on in the gears of her mind. We reviewed her basic psychology, as well as what changes in her body seem to be causing sudden meltdowns and unusual behavior. By now, hopefully, you have gained a stronger understanding of why your daughter may seem to act out as she does.

This understanding is the ground floor for the most important part of your journey to repair your relationship: action.

In this chapter, we will finally home in on how you can better connect with your daughter, working from the ground up to rebuild that sense of innate connection that you may have lost as your daughter grew from a child into a young woman. The next few pages will deep dive into what exactly it means to feel a "connection" like this, as well as steps you can take towards truly getting to know your daughter as the young woman she is becoming.

Without further ado, roll up your sleeves and prepare for the hard—but rewarding—work of reconnecting one of the most important relationships of any mother's life.

What is Connection?

Not long after Carol and Sarah's "date," Carol was up on a Saturday morning, finishing a bit of laundry she had let pile up throughout the week. She had just separated the denim when she noticed a folded piece of paper sticking up out of the pocket of one of Sarah's jeans. Curious, she took it out.

The blue-lined notebook paper had been folded into a tight little square, the edges soft from having rubbed against the inside of Sarah's tiny pocket. Shining through the thin paper, Carol could barely make out the imprint of words written in blue ink. She was just about to unfold the paper when she saw the boy's name written on the outside and realized with shock that this note was from Sarah's crush.

As tempting as it was to open the paper and learn what was going on in her daughter's personal life, Carol resisted the urge. Instead, she checked the time, poured an extra cup of coffee, and left the note on the counter for Sarah to find.

When Sarah woke up and came into the kitchen, her eyes almost immediately found the note. She made a beeline for the counter and tucked the square of paper into the pocket of her robe, her face already flushed with embarrassment.

Carol tried to stay as casual as possible. "What's that?" she asked.

Sarah walked to the coffee pot and fixed her usual: half coffee, half milk, with three spoons full of sugar. "Nothing," she muttered, "just a note. I don't know how that got there."

Carol considered the best way to phrase it. "I found it in your pocket when I was doing the laundry," she said, quickly adding, "I only thought you might not want it to get destroyed in the wash."

Sarah's eyes flashed with panic, and before she could ask, Carol said, "I didn't read it, I promise."

Sarah stood in the doorway like a frightened animal, as if she were about to walk away. Finally, she returned to her spot at the kitchen table, where she scrolled through her phone and sipped her lukewarm coffee. Carol sat across from her and waited hopefully, quietly thinking that her daughter might add something to this conversation. She wanted to pepper Sarah with questions: who was that boy? When did he give her that note? Was this the one she really liked or was it just a coincidence? Have they been talking?

Sarah continued to scroll through her phone, liking pictures on Instagram and avoiding her mother's gaze at all costs. When she finally glanced up, Carol sensed a nervousness behind her eyes that made it clear that she had no plans on continuing this conversation. Within a few minutes, Sarah sat up, stretched, and awkwardly said, "I'm going to go watch TV." She walked away, leaving her mother sitting silently in place, wondering what she had done wrong.

Carol thought for a moment about their last good day together. Then, it felt as if she and Sarah were finally starting to make headway in their relationship. It felt as if, after all their fighting, they were finally coming to a place of resolution. Now, sitting across from her daughter, she felt once more as if she were in the presence of a stranger.

For what felt like the hundredth time, Carol thought about the idea of connection. How was it possible that she so often felt as if she were living with a stranger? How was it that she knew exactly how Sarah had taken her coffee since she was just a kid when Carol insisted she only drink decaffeinated brews, yet she had no idea what was actually going on in her mind half the time? Feeling defeated, Carol got up, downed the last of her coffee, and went back to the laundry room, lost in her thoughts.

It's impossible to truly put the feeling of "connection" into words, but when you feel it, you just know. Conversation flows easily and never gets boring. You trust them with the deepest parts of yourself, and you know that, while you are with them, you are safe. They fit into your life as easily as one puzzle piece into another, as if you truly were made for each other, and you feel as if they see you as you actually are. In the best cases, they even introduce you to new levels of yourself, parts of your mind you never even knew.

At its core, a connection is about intimacy. It is about that feeling—warranted or not—that we truly stand a chance to know someone at their core. Though it may feel innate, a connection does not often come with a second's glace; it is built through a system of vulnerability and work.

Think back to when you and your daughter felt closest, to a time when you truly felt as if you could read her mind. Chances are, your mind may have shot back to when she was a little girl, fully enamored and dependent on you for all her needs.

In other words, when she was at her most vulnerable.

Now that your daughter is getting older, that innate vulnerability is quickly vanishing into independence. As she navigates the world on her own, the simple truth is that she no longer needs you in the same way that she once did. When that vulnerability vanishes, so may much of the connection that you felt between yourself and your daughter.

This is not to say that the connection is gone forever; it just takes a bit more work.

In the absence of physical vulnerability, you need to build a level of safe, non-judgmental, emotional vulnerability between you and your daughter. Only then can you actually grow to understand one another with the respect of two adults looking out for one another. Only then can you once again feel as if you know her from the inside out.

Here is the thing about emotional vulnerability, though: it is a two-way street.

Unfortunately, it is not going to be as easy as walking up to your daughter and demanding that she tell you all her secrets. In the same way, you have to remember that there is a difference between building trusting respect with your daughter and simply emotionally dumping on her. You are still a role model in her life, and as such, you want to serve as a model for the relationship you hope you will gain.

Instead of building an emotional connection by confessing all your secrets, instead, treat your relationship like an investment.

Not sure where to start?

Don't worry. I've got you covered.

Time

How often has your daughter heard you complain about time? How you wish you had more of it, how you don't know where it went? How often have you said the phrase, "That was a waste of time" when frustrated over something that did not go her way?

These words may be nothing more than a throwaway moment in your mind, but to her, they linger. She remembers them and internalizes the way that "time" creates stress in your life. Whether you like it or not, she adopts those same feelings of stress, rush, and anxiety in her own life, modeling your feelings to create a situation in which she always feels as behind as you do. In the worst cases, she looks at her own needs as similar "wastes of time," using those words as a reason not to come to you with her wants and needs.

The first real step to building a connection with your daughter is to show her that her needs are never a waste of your time.

The unfortunate truth is that, when life gets busy, it is easy for us to feel as if we won't have time to invest nearly as much as we want into the people we most care about. It feels as if we are just barely staying ahead of the chase, always falling further behind.

Be completely honest with yourself. How often have you sat across from your loved ones, smiling and nodding as if you were listening when your mind was circulating over all the things you could be getting done?

To make sure that you actually do have time to fully invest in your relationship with your daughter, take control of how you spend your time and start building routines that provide meaningful space for real, undistracted connection.

To start this process, consider the advice of expert time management strategists and perform a time audit (How to do a time audit).

As the name suggests, a time audit is a detailed analysis of what activities are taking up the most time in your day. By putting forth the effort to actually understand where your time is going, you can better decide how to move forward with a better plan of action.

To start this process, divide your usual activities into categories. This can be done however you please, but I suggest using the following format: work, chores, "maintenance," relaxation, and "time wasters."

The first two categories of this list are simple. Work and chores are both vital parts of keeping life running, and you should likely only reexamine the time you spend here if you realize that a push towards perfection is holding you back from the time that could be spent with your family. For example, if an analysis of your time shows that you are spending a full six hours every single week sweeping, mopping, and vacuuming, maybe you should consider accepting a slightly dirtier floor in exchange for a more relaxed family.

In my audit, the "maintenance" category holds all the things that simply have to be done for me to be my happiest, healthiest self. This includes cooking and eating, time in the gym, sleep, and any necessary doctor's appointments.

The final two categories are where the organization can get a little tricky. Relaxation comprises any activities that help you mentally recharge, while "time wasters" are activities that actually only drain your mental reserves.

By this point, we have discussed the idea of healthy self-care in detail. You have a thorough understanding of how important it is to invest time in caring for your mental health, both for your sake and for that of your daughter. While the relaxation category of your time audit holds all these vital self-care needs—reading, meditating, time in the bath, or spent with loved ones—the time wasters are all those easy activities that we find ourselves doing, then feeling guilty afterward. Think about how much time you spend on social media, scrolling through YouTube, or mindlessly isolating yourself in front of a sitcom you aren't really interested in watching, your phone in one hand as you further divide your own attention.

By taking an audit of how much time you truly spend in each category, you can better plan your day in a way that avoids these "time wasters" and instead reinvests those hours into time better spent. Rather than waking up at five am and spending an hour on Instagram, choose to give yourself than extra thirty minutes of sleep. Instead of sitting through a hundredth viewing of *The Big Bang Theory*, take time to schedule a weekly family movie night.

If you know that you are already utilizing your time as well as possible and still struggle to find space for those important relationships, think of ways you can integrate those relationships into your already busy schedule. Rather than doing the chores in isolation, consider turning them into a group activity; bring all the laundry into the living room to fold together. Make your daughter's sole chore responsibility the dishes, so that she can clean while you finish the after-dinner chores. Invite her to help you cook at least one meal a week, guaranteeing some quality time together while also teaching her a valuable life skill.

How you spend your time is how you spend your life. Take control of your time, model healthy living to your daughter, and remove the stress she may secretly be feeling over wasting your time with her problems. In doing so, you can open the door to better, deeper conversations, more emotional vulnerability, and a truly connected lifestyle.

Going on Dates

Now that you've completed a full, thorough audit of your time, it's time to move on to the next step: arranging regularly scheduled mother/daughter dates.

All too often, it is easy to categorize the relationship you share with your daughter as something unlike any other in your life. In many ways, it may truly be, but in truth, it falls victim to the same poor effects if you allow it to go neglected.

Think of it this way: would you spend time with a friend who consistently ignores you? Is it easy to maintain a romantic relationship with any person who never puts forth an effort to see you or spend time with you?

Why would the relationship with your daughter be any different?

Though you may see your daughter more often than any of your friends or even your romantic partner, this time only counts if it is purposeful, planned, and treated like the investment that it is. To show your daughter how important she is to your life, sit down with a calendar and come up with a schedule for "dates" you can take together. Even if these dates only occur once a month, make sure that she understands how you see them as a priority and follow through on that promise. Once these dates have been scheduled, no work conflicts, emergency meetings, or appointments can get in the way.

Even if the date itself is not likely to take longer than an afternoon, you'll be surprised to find how close the act of planning these dates is likely to bring you. By opening the door to planning any kind of event with your daughter, you are agreeing to an exchange of ideas, a chance to learn from one another, and a deeper exchange of priorities. To turn this into even more of a learning experience, consider giving your daughter a budget for this date. Whatever does not get spent on one date can be allotted to an even more expensive date next time. Sit back and watch how invested she gets in the process of researching ticket prices, menu options, and the cost of gas. Whether your daughter is more likely to debate in favor of a single hour at an expensive restaurant or an entire afternoon spent at a "pick it yourself" farm, you are sure to learn more about how she views her own time and money in the process.

Need help coming up with ideas? Check out a few of these options and discuss the possibilities with your daughter.

- A nature hike at a nearby trail
- A trip to the spa
- A walk through the strangest museum within 100 miles
- A full tea party, complete with fancy treats and guests
- A professional photoshoot
- A shopping spree
- Finding and tackling a new Pinterest project
- Going fishing
- A full day of thrifting
- Dinner at a restaurant neither of you has tried

- A two-day road trip to a city you haven't seen before

As the clock counts down to your date, find ways to sprinkle reminders throughout the days leading up to the event. Leave sticky notes on her bathroom mirror counting down to your adventure, plan themed snacks, and if necessary, build up to the event by getting supplies together.

However you decide to do it, make sure that your daughter understands how excited you are to spend this valuable time with her.

Understanding their Interests

Sometimes, speaking to your daughter about her interests can feel a little like trying to read a book in a language you barely understand. Though all the words may individually make sense, as a whole they leave you clueless.

Learning to understand your daughter's interests may not be an easy task, and it is certainly not one that can be tackled overnight. It is going to take consistent effort, an open mind, and lots of time on your part, but the overall effects are well worth it.

Depending on how talkative your daughter naturally is, you may not even have the chance to simply ask her about these interests in the way you might approach an

adult. Any attempt to ask her directly about her musical taste, hobbies, or general interests may only put her on guard, making her
feel as if you are prying into her personal life. Only you know whether a direct approach would be best, but in most cases, I recommend an alternative: observation.

Think about some of the moments in your own life in which you felt the most seen and understood. Chances are, these moments didn't spring out of a conversation in which someone asked you about those interests. Rather, it's likely that the greatest feelings of warmth and happiness came from knowing that this person paid attention although you never put a voice to your thoughts on the subject.

It's one thing when someone asks you your favorite flavor of ice cream; it's a whole other level of appreciation when someone notices your love of spicy flavors, and then surprises you with a unique pint of "Mexican Hot Chocolate" ice cream they saw at the store.

In much the same way, showing your daughter your love and appreciation through the act of giving your attention is likely enough to make up for any feelings that you are too "behind on the times" to understand her.

At this stage in her life, your daughter is likely in a stage of constant experimentation. As she attempts to determine her place in the world, she may cycle through a variety of different aesthetics and tastes. By sifting through different personalities, she is crying out to find out which world best seems to help her feel like "herself." In doing so, she unintentionally makes it incredibly easy to identify what easy outlets for understanding and easy conversation.

An easy place to start is with her social media.

Every generation of teenagers has idolized their own version of pop stars, actors, or other leaders, but this generation's idolization enters a different kind of level. In the push for authenticity and the ever-present call of social media, your daughter may feel as if she knows her idols on an even deeper level than you might have imagined based on your own experiences. She does not just know their music; she knows their thoughts, feelings, and political views. Based on their activity, she may know what the inside of their house or the structure of their family is like. What's more, in the age of the internet, your daughter's favorite "celebrities" may not even be people that you would initially consider celebrities at all! Through the power of Instagram, TikTok, and YouTube, everyday teenagers and young adults find themselves shot into the spotlight, where they serve as a different kind of idol for the younger generation.

If you find yourself clueless about where to start in learning more about your daughter's interests and hobbies, start by looking at what her favorite YouTubers and TikTokers are doing. Chances are high that if she has begun styling herself after her favorite artist on TikTok, your daughter is finding an interest in art; once you notice that she has picked up the popular phrases of an athlete she admires, look into more of what this athlete "stands for" to find out more about the kinds of interests that are currently catching your daughter's eye.

In the best-case scenario, this extra investigation might lead you to a deeper understanding of the kinds of art, music, and activities that bring your daughter her deepest joy.

In the worst-case scenario, she is still likely to see—potentially roll her eyes at—and appreciate the effort you are putting forth.

Managing Conflict

If the key to connection truly lies in creating a safe place for your daughter to be vulnerable, you must learn the strategies you need to navigate the conflicts that are sure to arise.

As you and your daughter venture into this uncharted territory, it is a guarantee that tensions are going to rise. The more she feels as if she thinks you may buck against her ideas or laugh at her interests, the more likely it is that she shut down entirely, cutting you off from the most intimate, vulnerable parts of her, the parts that are unfortunately most important in building the kind of connection you need for your relationship to thrive. This being said, you are still the adult, and no matter how old she may feel, she is still just a child. You are not doing your daughter any favors simply by allowing her to have her way just for the sake of keeping things easy.

It may feel like a tricky balance, but to keep the peace while still guiding your daughter on the right path, you need to establish clear, firm boundaries and guard them without anger or judgment.

A boundary is more than just a rule; it is a guideline for how the two of you will relate to one another, and as such, you need to be sure that your daughter understands that she cannot simply push this boundary and get her way.

Think back to the introduction of this book, in which we saw one of Carol and Sarah's earlier, more explosive fights. In this situation, Sarah—acting out of frustration and hurt—pushed back against her mother. This was her testing the boundary that had become an unspoken part of their relationship, the boundary that stated she was supposed to follow her mother's guidelines regarding cleanliness. Carol—again, acting out of frustration and hurt—pushed back even further, responding out of anger rather than empathy. This led the argument to grow, culminating in Sarah calling her mother a hurtful name and storming from the room.

Take a moment and try to identify Carol's biggest issue here.

By now, hopefully, you understand what a grave error she made in responding to Sarah's sass with a heated, angry tone. Though at that moment, Carol was only trying to have her own voice heard, she accidentally set a new standard in the relationship, one that reads in Sarah's mind as if she does not need to respect her mother whenever she feels disrespected. To add insult to injury, Sarah now understands that all she needs to do to hurt her mother is react in this same exact way, resorting to name-calling just to get a reaction.

After learning more about conflict resolution, Carol understood how differently she should have handled this sensitive situation.

Rather than coming at her daughter with a tone of exhaustion, she should have reminded her that her backpack does not belong in the middle of the floor. When Sarah mentioned her plan to clean after she had taken a moment to relax, Carol should have accepted this, then given Sarah a clear time limit by which point the chore should be completed. Whenever it was clear that she had accidentally let the dog out, Carol could have taken this in stride. Instead of screaming, she should have just said that accidents happen—because really, who hasn't made a simple mistake like this out of exhaustion?—and told Sarah that she now needed to wash the dog to recover from this mistake.

Conflict resolution can often feel like an art. Much like any art, though, it can easily be improved on through practice, even if it does not feel the most natural in the world.

In moments where you feel the tension rising between you and your daughter, don't allow hurt feelings to damage the growth you have already made in your relationship. Instead, consider a few of these tips from the experts at UC Berkley (13):

- Let your daughter express her feelings
- Listen openly
- Be sure you understand what the core of the problem is
- Actively look for a solution that you both can understandably live with
- Ideally, make sure that your daughter feels as if she has a role in this solution-finding process.

Before allowing this conflict to blow up into something more significant, ask yourself one final question: does this really matter?

In the end, what is the problem with a few tiny mistakes here and there? It's easy to worry that they might be indicative of some kind of deeper flaw—laziness, inattention to detail, procrastination—that you need to encourage your daughter to steer clear of, but in truth aren't we all victims to these little errors every once in a while?

Chances are, whatever topic seems so vital to addressing now may not feel the same way in the morning. Really consider what the consequences would be if this topic went unaddressed. In the end, you may find that, as long as no one is being disrespected, hurt, or neglected, the conflict itself may be better left alone for the sake of peace in your household.

In Summary

Ultimately, as much as we like to think that connections happen instantly and automatically, they often take time and effort. As your daughter grows from the vulnerable child she once was into an independently thinking young woman, you may feel as if the connection that once came so naturally is slipping through your fingertips. In truth, this simply means that you can no longer depend on the same vulnerability that once linked every small, helpless child to their caregivers. Instead, you know how to create a safe space for the emotional vulnerability your daughter needs to feel as if she can trust you with her feelings.

To build this connection, take an active role in your relationship. Invest your time in her, serving as a model for how she should set her own future priorities. Be sure that you are taking time to spend one-on-one with one another. Build "mother-daughter dates" into your regular routine, and invite her to join you in planning the kind of fun, lively experiences that build connection. Take the same manner of approach towards conflict solving. Instead of telling her the rules as they must be followed, build healthy boundaries and model how to react when those boundaries are pushed. In the face of conflict, always remember: the problem is the enemy, not your daughter.

Application Workbook 5

As you work to build this connection, continue trying the following:

- **Schedule weekly dinners and institute a "no phones policy"** at the table. To really work, this rule should apply to everyone in the household, parents included!
- Consider **only allowing television in common areas of the house**. This will help in two ways: limiting screen time and encouraging family togetherness.
- **Create a welcoming environment for your daughter's friends**. Keep the cabinets stocked with snacks and do what you can to incorporate your daughter's friends into the household routine.

Step 6: Working Together

For whatever reason, it is easy to forget that the relationship between a mother and daughter is just that: a relationship. As such, it takes care, nurturing, and an element of work to keep it healthy and functioning. Because the people involved in this relationship are still humans—with conflicting thoughts, feelings, and desires—it can't be exempt from the kinds of problems that cause issues in any dynamic. Where the challenge comes is how those issues are handled.

If you and a coworker were to encounter repeated arguments over how to handle a problem in your workplace, what would you do? Likely, you probably would not want to quit your job and start someplace new over this issue, especially knowing that these kinds of problems are inevitable. Instead, you would accept the challenge, have a mature conversation, and find ways around this issue by working together, as a team.

Whenever similar issues arise in your relationship with your daughter, there is good news; because you are already working from such a solid foundation, you are already halfway there!

In this last chapter, let's turn back to Carol and Sarah as they demonstrate the exact methods that I most suggest in turning a strained, painful relationship into one united through hard work and dedication to a shared goal.

Power of Listening Effectively

"Hey Sarah, did you look over that list of ideas I sent you?"

Carol knocked twice and waited for a response before entering Sarah's bedroom. Sarah lay on her stomach across the bed, pouring over the last bit of her homework for the day. She was still struggling in math, but Carol was proud to see that she was clearly making an effort toward getting better.

"Yeah, about that..." Sarah spun around and faced her mother, with an uncomfortable, tense expression on her face. Carol felt her stomach drop.

"What? What's the problem?"

"I just looked at that list of stuff you left out, and honestly, it all just looked kind of... lame."

Carol felt the heat rise to her face, then felt even more embarrassed that she would allow a teenage girl to make her so embarrassed. Determined to follow through on her "daughter date" idea, Carol had spent her entire lunch break researching things for her and Sarah to do. When she first brought the idea up, she could tell Sarah seemed hesitant, but she was hoping that after she looked at the fun list that Carol had brainstormed, she might come around.

"What was so lame about it?" Carol asked.

Sarah shrugged. "I don't know. Just none of that stuff seemed cool. Like, I honestly just don't want to spend my Saturday walking around some musty museum. And have you felt this weather lately? I'm not getting out and going on some hike." She shrugged again. "You get it, right?"

Carol nodded, trying not to feel completely defeated. "That's fine," she said, then started to turn from the room. At the last minute, something inside of her gave her pause. She turned back around and sat on the end of Sarah's bed, pulling the laptop towards her.

"Actually, do you mind if we research a few things we could do instead, then?"

Sarah blinked in surprise, but then she nodded. Carol asked her permission before opening her laptop and clicking the space bar, waking up the sleeping screen. The monitor brightly lit up the corner of the room, and on the screen, Carol saw that Sarah had paused in the middle of an interview with Megan Rapinoe.

"Oh my gosh, I forgot that she existed," Carol said.

Sarah laughed at added, "I almost did too. She's not a big deal anymore, I don't think, but I really like the way she talks about things."

"What do you mean?"

"Like, I don't know. It just seems like she really cares about stuff that not a lot of other people are talking about.

Like, did you know that the US women's soccer team still makes way less than the guy's soccer team, even though they bring more fans to the seats? That's just not fair."

"Yeah, I remember a few years back she was in the news all the time."

Sarah nodded. "This is one of her interviews from back then. Just look at how this guy talks to her." Sarah clicked play on the video but then proceeded to talk over the interviewers. Carol had to suppress a laugh whenever Sarah asked her a question and then carried on without waiting for an answer.

In Carol's pocket, her phone began vibrating. A quick glance down at the screen showed that her sister was calling, likely looking for an update on how the mother-daughter date plan was going.

When Sarah saw the phone in her mother's hand she paused. "Is it getting too late? I know you're busy," she said.

Carol put the phone away, scooted closer to her daughter and said, "Not at all, baby. Now, what was it you were saying about that Medal of Freedom?"

They sat there for another twenty minutes, following one video link after another but never even opening another window to research date ideas.

The next day, Carol came home to find a handwritten list of alternative date ideas on the refrigerator, the top idea—a trip to a professional soccer game—was highlighted in yellow.

Judge Less

Four days from their date night—they finally decided on a traditional movie and dinner—Carol came home later than usual. A work meeting had run later than expected, and on the way home, she had called Sarah to let her know that she would be picking up dinner for both of them. Personally, Carol hated Buffalo Wild Wings, but knowing it was Sarah's favorite, she drove the additional twenty minutes and waited on a sticky, smelly bench for their to-go order. The noise gave her a massive headache, but she had forgotten to refill the usual stash of Advil she tucked away in her purse. By the time she arrived home, she was exhausted, stressed, and struggling against the start of a nasty migraine.

When she saw the empty frozen pizza box still sitting on the counter, it was all she could take not to lose it.

She dropped her purse at the bar and took a long, deep breath before calling Sarah's name.

Sarah bounced into the room seconds later, still nibbling on the extra large slice of pepperoni and sausage pizza.

"Hey, Mom," she said, "What's up?"

"What's up?" Carol said, "I thought I told you that I was picking up dinner for tonight."

Sarah glanced at the huge to-go bag now sitting on the counter. "Oh nice, Buffalo Wild Wings," she said, "I'm full now, but you can have my share if you want."

"I don't especially want any share of this," Carol said, "I got this for you." She looked around the kitchen, noting the pile of dirty dishes still in the sink and Sarah's backpack thrown in that same corner Carol repeatedly told her not to use. She bit her tongue to resist the urge to scream at her.

"Sarah," she finally said, "I am completely exhausted. The last thing I wanted to come home to was a mess."

Sarah's face flushed bright red in response, and Carol was surprised to see tears welling up in the corners of her eyes. Before the fight could escalate any further, she said, "You know what, enjoy your pizza. We can talk about his later."

Sarah nodded her head and left the room.

To help herself unwind, Carol ran a hot bath and nibbled at her plate of now lukewarm fries in the tub, a cool rag draped over her eyes to take away the sting of her headache. As her headache faded, so did much of her annoyance. By the time she wrapped up in a towel and went back to the kitchen, she was able to look at the situation with new eyes.

Sure, Sarah's backpack had been thrown in the corner of the room, but her math textbook was also on the kitchen table. She must have gotten to work as soon as she got home and simply forgotten to put away all her assignments. With a pang of guilt, Carol also noticed her own purse still thrown across the counter, taking up just as much space as the backpack she had come so close to fighting with her daughter over. Carol glanced over the work and breathed a sigh of relief that she would never have to take another math class again.

When Carol looked at the counter, she saw that Sarah had thrown the pizza box away. She also remembered the text that Sarah had sent her just yesterday, asking her to pick up a new box of tampons. Once again, her period had unexpectedly started four days early. Sarah had only gotten her first period less than a year ago, and in the newness, she had yet to figure out how to plan around it. Once again, Carol felt a pang of guilt as she realized that Sarah, cramping and exhausted, had probably just fallen victim to the same cravings that sent her running to the store for ice cream once a month.

Three minutes later, Carol was knocking on the door to Sarah's bedroom, apologizing for her actions and asking her to join her for an episode of *Friends* before they both went to bed.

It's easy when we are caught up in the swell of our own problems to judge the mistakes of our daughters. After all, it's human nature. When someone causes an inconvenience to your already stressful day, the easier option is always going to be to fall victim to the judgments that come so naturally.

Whenever you feel yourself judging your daughter too harshly—thinking of her as lazy or inconsiderate—do what you would want others to do for you. Take a step back and reexamine the situation with fresh eyes. Ask yourself: does this problem matter? Are these mistakes I have not made myself?

Remember, reserving judgments and extending grace is always the better option in smoothing out a rocky relationship and working together towards a better future.

More Supporters, Not Dictators

Three days before their date night, Carol was sitting in her bedroom, paying a few bills, when she got an email from Sarah's math teacher. Carol had been in communication with this teacher for the last two weeks, as they worked together to monitor Sarah's struggling math grade. This new email was good news; though Sarah was still struggling to focus in class, her consistent homework grades were helping to slowly raise her average. Not only that, but her most recent test score showed an improvement by a full letter grade.

Carol went to Sarah's room, expecting to find her finishing her homework. Instead, she found her sitting on the floor, scrolling through her phone. The math homework lay on the bed, still half finished.

"Hey," Carol said, "What are you up to?"

"Just taking a break," Sarah said, "Why?"

Carol sat on the edge of Sarah's bed and skimmed through the half-finished worksheet. "It's already nine o'clock," she said, "Don't you think you need to get this done so you can go to bed?"

Sarah rolled her eyes. "I will, I promise," she said. "I'm just taking a little break."

Carol looked over Sarah's shoulder and saw that she was skimming through that she was messaging that boy from her math class, the one she knew was already such a distraction.

"Sarah, I just got another email from your teacher. He said that your grade is going up, but it's almost entirely because your homework grades are making up for the lower classwork scores. It really is important that you get this done before you get too tired. These grades matter."

"I'm just taking a break. I've been at it for an hour," Sarah said, half paying attention as she replied to an incoming message, "I let myself take a fifteen-minute break for every hour of work I do. It's part of the process."

For a minute, Carol had to fight the urge to grab the phone from her daughter's hand. Then, she took a long breath and remembered to ask herself: how much does this matter?

At Sarah's age, her credits would not affect her high school GPA for another year. Her teacher had admitted that she had been showing improvement, and for weeks, Sarah had been completing her homework without Carol breathing down her neck to get it done. Even if Carol took her phone and insisted that she finish all her work, what good would come from that helicopter parenting? Would Sarah learn that much from the interaction, or would it just create more problems down the road?

"Alright," Carol finally said, "Enjoy your break, but remember, I fully expect you to maintain at least a B average in this class. It may not seem important, but math is an especially hard class to catch up on once you let yourself fall behind. Even if it doesn't feel like it matters now, you need this class to do well in next year's math class and every class after that."

Boundaries VS Free Reign

Before moving forward with Carol and Sarah's story, I think it is important to take a moment and review a key point of the interaction above: the difference between setting a boundary and allowing your daughter free reign.

No matter who we are, life hands us a natural set of boundaries. The boundaries dictate what manner of behavior is healthy, reinforced by the natural consequences of a poor decision.

For example, when our impulse is to stay up for hours past our bedtime binging a new television show, the natural boundary life hands us reminds us that work requires us to be up by a certain time. Whenever we cross that boundary and do as we please, we suffer a natural consequence: exhaustion, crankiness, or tardiness in our workplace.

Boundaries are about more than just rules; they are about health and safety, as well as judging what is in our long-term best interests. When deciding what boundaries are worth setting for your daughter, come back to this rule. Think about what is in her long-term best interest. Clearly communicate an expectation and allow her the freedom to find ways to reach that expectation.

In telling Sarah what her grading expectations were and explaining why she held that standard, Carol was doing more than telling her daughter what to do. She was setting a boundary, then allowing her daughter the freedom to meet that boundary in a way that worked best for her.

For parents who take a more authoritative approach or insist on "calling the shots," this interaction may have made Carol look weak, as if she were allowing her daughter free reign. In actuality, she was simply picking her battles and taking an objective look at what could have otherwise been a heated situation.

When navigating the tricky waters of parenting a teenage girl, it's vital to learn how and when to pick these battles. If necessary, try to look at the situation not as a mother, but as a casual observer. Ask yourself if this is a matter of safety, as well as if there are any major consequences to this minor issue.

In the end, Carol made the right decision. Rather than acting as a dictator, insisting that her daughter follow her exact orders in the very minute that she gave them, she took a step back, evaluated the situation, and decided to give her daughter freedom.

Ultimately, it was the best possible decision.

Can you guess why?

In the end, Sarah went to sleep without finishing her homework. The next day, she struggled during a pop quiz reviewing the skills she did not practice well enough. The next time she found herself distracted by her phone, she remembered that pop quiz, felt a healthy pang of annoyance, and pushed through the distractions to finish her work on time.

By allowing Sarah the freedom to make her own tiny mistakes, Carol gives her daughter a gift: the chance to learn from the natural consequences of her own actions.

Teach Life Skills

Two days before their scheduled date, Sarah walked into the kitchen just as Carol was starting to do the dishes.

"Hey, Mom, can I run something by you?"

"Sure, baby. What's going on?"

Sarah pulled up a chair and sat at the island bar as Carol finished washing the zucchini for their dinner. "Well, I was thinking about our date night."

"Are you excited for it?"

"Yeah, I mean, I am…" Carol sensed that Sarah was not saying something. Rather than pushing for a response, she allowed the silence to rest between them until Sarah spoke again. "It's just, I don't know if dinner is the best idea."

"Don't you think now is a little late to start backing out? I already made reservations," Carol said.

"Hear me out," Sarah said, "Do you remember how you gave me that budget? When you told me to pick out something for us to do, I mean."

"Yeah, I remember."

"Well, I've been doing a little research, and I think instead of getting dinner, I'd rather save that money and do something a little bigger next month."

"Yeah? Like what?" Carol fumbled with the vegetables and cutting board, distracted.

"Do you know that band you asked me about? The one with that blue-haired girl?"

Carol nodded. In trying to learn more about Sarah's interests, she had begun letting her control the music on the way to and from school. Most of the singers still sounded like screeching cats, but they had found common ground in one folk singer. Her deep, gravelly voice reminded Carol a bit of Stevie Nicks from her Fleetwood Mac days. Carol took the chance to show Sarah their *Rumors* album, and "Landslide" had jumped the list to become one of Sarah's top ten favorite songs of all time.

Sarah continued, "She's playing in a city not too far from here in two months. It's, like, an hour's drive. I thought if we skipped dinner this time, we could save that money to use next month and make a bigger event out of seeing her together."

Carol immediately warmed to the idea. "I like this a lot," she said, "but how much money would we save just by skipping dinner? Wouldn't it be better to miss the movie instead?"

"But I really, really wanted to see that movie!" Sarah said.

"Which is more important, the concert or the movie?"

Sarah thought for a minute. "The concert would be more fun," she said carefully, "But I was looking forward to a movie night. What if instead of going to the movies, we rented a new release to stream at home?"

Carol nodded in agreement. "Tell me more about this concert," she added, "Where exactly is it? What is the venue? Is it a bar?"

When Sarah could not give her a full answer, Carol told her to grab her laptop and look up more information about the venue. She navigated the website alongside her daughter, showing her how to use the "Earth View" of Google Maps to check out the neighborhood. The venue was a bar after all, but because this singer had such a young fanbase, she was offering an early show that promised not to be nearly as rowdy. Before grabbing her credit card, Carol pointed out that, with a drive this long, Sarah may have to miss soccer practice the evening after the show. Sarah committed to texting the coach in advance about her possible absence and staying late at the following practice to run the extra drills. Carol went ahead and purchased tickets, asking Sarah to chop the vegetables as she did.

Taken at face value, this interaction may have appeared incredibly simple, just a mother and daughter in conversation about their plans. A closer look under the surface, however, will prove that this interaction was far more valuable.

Within a brief conversation, Carol:

- Modeled time management, asking that her daughter help with the research rather than placing the burden solely on her mother, who was busy cooking
- Respect for authority figures, guiding Sarah to inform her coach in advance about the missed practice and her plans to recover the lost time
- Computer skills, showing her how to use the internet to navigate their safety
- Budgeting, as Sarah debated the benefits of skipping dinner versus missing the movie

If you have any experience with teenagers, you already know that dictating life lessons to them can feel like a wasted effort. Their natural drive for independence and general state of distraction can lead to only feeling offense at your efforts to "tell them what to do." Rather than trying to force your ideal and life lessons onto your child, find the opportunities within your regular interactions to teach them the vital skills you know they need as they navigate life.

This rule falls back on the same principle that can make "helicopter parenting" such a dangerous trap. It's easy to tell your child what to do, but often, this manner of coddling only dampens their own sense of independence, serving to hold them back later in life.

Don't attempt to force your daughter in whatever direction you think she should follow; instead, guide her. Lead by example, and allow her to learn life's lessons along the way, as naturally as any adult continues their own path towards growth.

Unconditional Love

After much anticipation, the day arrived: the long-awaited, heavily planned, first-ever mother-daughter date.

And it could not have possibly been more of a disaster.

Sarah had taken so long getting ready that they had to race out of the door thirty full minutes after expected, leading to their being fully caught in the throws of rush-hour traffic. In her desperation to make the reservation, Carol was pulled over and given a speeding ticket. By the time they finally made it to their restaurant, they had fully missed their reservation and were asked to wait in a long line of other impatient diners. With not enough benches to go around, Carol had to stand, her heels rubbing a deeper blister into the back of her heel by the second.

Almost two full hours after expected, they were finally seated and given their menus. In her hunger and annoyance, Sarah had already looked through the menu online and decided what she wanted. For the entire wait, she had joked about how much better that giant plate of chicken parmesan was going to taste after standing for so long. As luck would have it, this was exactly the dish that the waiter told them was sold out for the evening.

Rather than picking another item from the menu, Sarah sulked for the entire first half of the meal. Carol, finally losing her temper, told her to "suck it up, buttercup," to which Sarah refused to speak to her the entire car ride home.

They finally walked through the door at nearly nine o'clock that evening. Without saying another word, Sarah stormed to her room and slammed the door behind her.

Carol gave her around thirty minutes to cool off.

Then, she followed her.

As usual, she knocked three times and waited for a response before coming in. She found Sarah laying face down on her bed, refusing to look at her. Carol crossed the room, sat on the far corner of the bed, and gently rubbed her daughter's back.

"I know you're disappointed about how our evening went," she said, "Honestly, I am too. I'm sorry I snapped at you. I'm sorry that so much of this evening just seemed determined to work against us. I'm still not sorry we went out together though. I had a lot of fun waiting in line for you, even if my hanger got the best of me."

From under her mess of hair, Sarah chuckled in spite of herself. Carol smiled, encouraged.

"If you want to make up for it at lunch tomorrow, let me know, and I'll clear my schedule. I'm about to go rent that movie if you feel up to joining me."

After a moment, Sarah nodded, sat up, and hugged her mom tight around the shoulders. Together, they went to finish their night together over a bowl of microwaved popcorn, determined to leave their date better than they had started it.

Unconditional love does not mean loving one another during the easy times. It doesn't look like effortless afternoons, sunny days, and easy mornings. If it did, it would not be half as remarkable as what it truly is: the combined decision to work at loving one another even through the tough times.

Unconditional love is exactly that. It is unconditional. It is free from the restraints of rules or logic. When romantic or platonic love shows up for the party, unconditional love is the kind that sticks around after the event to help clean up. It is the love that comes to the doorstep every single day without fail, whether you are tired or hungry or cranky or giddy.

In his book *For One More Day,* Mitch Albom wrote, "When you look into your mother's eyes, you know that it is the purest love you can find on this earth."

To show your daughter that the love you have for her is truly unconditional, you have to do more than plan fun nights together. You have to be there, free from judgement or criticism, when those plans inevitably fall through. In choosing forgiveness and laughter in the face of failure, you are doing something so much more than just making light of a problem. You are reinforcing in her mind the confidence that tells her, no matter what happens, she can still turn to you in times of need.

In Summary

The act of repairing a difficult relationship takes more than just a single person; it is a team effort. However, unlike in other relationships in your life, it's key to remember that in this instance, your partner is still just a child. As the adult, you may need to prepare to lead this effort for as long as it takes for her to relax, learn to trust you, and fall into the rhythm that you are building within your relationship.

To help your daughter feel as if you are approaching her from a place of love rather than control, practice actively listening to her thoughts and opinions. Take the lessons of the last few chapters, and put them to work by taking an active role in learning more about your daughter's interests. As you do, show compassion and refrain from judging the differences in your tastes. Your daughter is in the midst of a vital stage in her development, and filtering through different "phases" is just another part of the process.

Rather than filling her life with rules, teach her that life comes with natural boundaries. Certain actions have consequences, and as long as what she is doing is not detrimental to her long-term health and goals, your daughter should experience these natural consequences for herself. Otherwise, the life lessons you hope to teach her will seem more like lectures than actual guidance.

As you and your daughter adjust to one another's changing needs, remember how important it is for you to actively show her your love throughout this process. Even when times feel tough, avoid allowing your own emotions to get the better of you. Instead, remind her that it is okay to feel angry, upset, and disappointed with the people you care about, and demonstrate that no mistakes she may make will ever change the unconditional love you carry in your heart for her.

Conclusion

At this point, you may be wondering about Carol and Sarah. What happened after that first disastrous date night? Where are they now? Did they ever heal their relationship?

The answer to these questions might be more complicated than you'd like to hear.

Because Carol and Sarah are compilations of different mothers and daughters I have spoken to over my years of experience, their story has one of many endings.

In some cases, "Carol and Sarah's" journey to healing is a smooth and easy one. They both jump into the challenge of connecting with one another, ready to work together and make a chance. They took the bad days alongside the good ones, and now they celebrate the kind of close relationship that most mothers only dream of having with their daughters.

In other cases, "Carol and Sarah" faced a bit more struggle. As two incredibly different individuals, they had a hard time ever seeing eye-to-eye. Communication didn't come easily, but by working on what they could control—respect, trust, and understanding—they were slowly able to build a friendship where there once was only fighting and chaos. In this version of events, they now look back on those days of arguments as if they were a joke, treating them as just a funny leg of their journey.

Unfortunately, not all problems end so happily.

Many of the "Carols" I have mentored over the years never learned how to relinquish that control. They continued to see the need for power in the relationship as more valuable than the need for understanding. Rather than trying to learn more about their daughter's interests, they continued to treat those interests as 'silly,' and in turn, the "Sarah's" in that world pushed back with every ounce of their energy. Instead of seeing their mothers as their biggest allies, they saw them only as enemies. They spent the majority of their teenage years hiding secrets from them, too worried about the anger and judgment they feared that they would face sharing their vulnerabilities.

Sometimes, time alone was enough to heal these sad cases; most of the time, it wasn't.

In the end, your relationship with your daughter is much like a "choose your own adventure" novel. Every time you reach a moment of potential conflict, you have the option to choose whatever option seems best at the time. Instead of turning to the page indicating more snark, impatience, or anger, do your best to choose the pages that show compassion.

Is the journey ahead likely an easy one? Absolutely not. However, empowered with the right information, you can now go forward with confidence, knowing that in each situation, you can make the best choices possible.

If this book has helped you in any way or improved your relationship with your daughter, please leave some positive feedback as it would mean the world to me. Thank you.

References:

Chapter One:

1. Leong, V., Byrne, E., Clackson, K., Georgieva, S., Lam, S., & Wass, S. (2017). Speaker gaze increases information coupling between infant and adult brains. Proceedings of the National Academy of Sciences, 114(50), 13290–13295. https://doi.org/10.1073/pnas.1702493114
2. Independent Digital News and Media. (2017, December 3). The 10 most difficult questions children ask parents. The Independent. Retrieved August 30, 2022, from https://www.independent.co.uk/news/uk/home-news/curious-children-questions-parenting-mum-dad-google-answers-inquisitive-argos-toddlers-chad-valley-tots-town-a8089821.html
3. A;, N. M. K. Y. S. (2008, February 15). The functional neuroanatomy of Maternal love: Mother's response to infant's attachment behaviors. Biological psychiatry. Retrieved September 1, 2022, from https://pubmed.ncbi.nlm.nih.gov/17686467/

Chapter Two:

4. Brain development in pre-teens and teenagers. Raising Children Network. (2021, April 23). Retrieved September 3, 2022, from https://raisingchildren.net.au/pre-teens/development/understanding-your-pre-teen/brain-development-teens
5. World Health Organization. (n.d.). Adolescent mental health. World Health Organization. Retrieved September

4, 2022, from https://www.who.int/news-room/fact-sheets/detail/adolescent-mental-health

Chapter Three:

6. Swamy, A. (2022, July 22). Helping your teen deal with the loss of a friendship. some useful tips and ways. ParentCircle. Retrieved September 19, 2022, from https://www.parentcircle.com/helping-teenage-deal-with-loss-of-a-friendship/article

7. Livingston, G. (2020, May 30). The way U.S. teens spend their time is changing, but differences between boys and girls persist. Pew Research Center. Retrieved September 19, 2022, from https://www.pewresearch.org/fact-tank/2019/02/20/the-way-u-s-teens-spend-their-time-is-changing-but-differences-between-boys-and-girls-persist/

Chapter Four:

8. Jeffreys, B. (2022, March 18). Girls face more pressure to be a perfect teenager. BBC News. Retrieved September 22, 2022, from https://www.bbc.com/news/education-60785871

9. Rampton, J. (2019, September 24). The science behind procrastination and how you'll beat it. Entrepreneur. Retrieved September 22, 2022, from https://www.entrepreneur.com/business-news/the-science-behind-procrastination-and-how-youll-beat-it/339801#:~:text=%22The%20limbic%20system%20is%20a,out%2C%20leading%20to%20procrastination.%22

10. Overview of Mood Disorders. Cedars-Sinai Health. (n.d.). Retrieved September 23, 2022, from https://www.cedars-sinai.org/health-library/diseases-and-conditions/o/overview-of-mood-disorders.html
11. Rise in prescription drug misuse and abuse impacting teens. SAMHSA. (n.d.). Retrieved September 24, 2022, from https://www.samhsa.gov/homelessness-programs-resources/hpr-resources/rise-prescription-drug-misuse-abuse-impacting-teens

Chapter Five:

12. How to do a time audit. Lucidchart. (2020, June 25). Retrieved October 8, 2022, from https://www.lucidchart.com/blog/how-to-do-a-time-audit#:~:text=Simply%20put%2C%20a%20time%20audit,want%20to%20spend%20your%20time.
13. Resolving conflict situations. Resolving Conflict Situations | People & Culture. (n.d.). Retrieved October 9, 2022, from https://hr.berkeley.edu/hr-network/central-guide-managing-hr/managing-hr/interaction/conflict/resolving